"Our dreams are fluid adventures of lifetimes, moments, and perceptions, as we have trouble separating the intervals of our reality"

IN SEARCH OF THE HEAVENS

AN INTROSPECTIVE ON SOULFUL EVOLUTION

MICHAEL ZEMBROWSKY

In Search of the Heavens

©2020, Michael Zembrowsky

ISBN: 978-1-09834-615-7
ISBN eBook: 978-1-09834-616-4

In memory of the following families:

Rosenthal, Cohen, Loeffler, Ziman,
Zembrowsky, Zagarowski, Greenberg, Wedeles,
Stein, Porges, Zak, Bleyer, Kohn, Roth, and Lederer

I have lived before…

CONTENTS

Dynamics of the Soul — Part C

AUTHORS FORWARD

As the casket was laid to the ground in the spring of 2001, there was a realization that I had been here once before. Rosehill Cemetery in Kansas City was reminiscent of all the times I ditched Sunday school, skipped over gravesites, and snuck off to the ethnic deli just beyond the wall.

This cemetery was a regular collection of who's who, within the Kansas City Jewish community. Often we played games counting names of people we recognized.

On this sad day, with the burial of my father, I looked off to the side. Adjacent to his plot was my grandmother's and step-grandfather's, once so influential in my early years. I looked to the east, and saw my other grandfather next to great aunts and uncles… A bit further, I noticed names that belonged to great grandparents, and distant cousins.

The graves reflected a story of immigration to the United States in the 1880s making their home in Kansas City, and creating an atmosphere of which I was groomed to reside. Voices passed through my head of all the conversations and discussions I once knew. There appears to be a bridge to my past, and it all started from the voices of others.

With the passing of my mother in 2011, I published a Genealogy book donated to libraries across the world. From my research, I found an ever expanding linkage to Europe, and the roots of my own personal DNA.

Kansas City has been the stage of my own reality. Born in 1957, I had the pleasure of growing up in the space age. "That of television, John Kennedy, and the Beatles...." Much inspiration was also driven from the Kansas City Chiefs and the science of our day.

Often I wondered how and why, I just happened to be born at this exact place in time, in consideration of the vast expanse of history. It is at this time I have derived my current reality.

Michael Zembrowsky was born and raised in Kansas City where he grew up among the tradition of three generations. Growing up in the Brookside area of Kansas City, Michael attended Shawnee Mission East High School in Prairie Village Kansas, and later the University of Kansas where he majored in Journalism. After years in the field of advertising, he now resides in Overland Park Kansas.

Inquiries can be made to *mike@rmsadvertising.com*

PREFACE

As I reflect on memories of my past, I recognize the presence of forces that have shadowed me throughout my life. I am guided by intuition and often fueled by awareness outside of my current condition.

During times of illness, I've experienced my body becoming somewhat diminished or "faded." Pain usually subsides, as a type of third party shroud overtakes my presence like a pulsing aura. Consciousness always remains intact, as I experience personas of outside vantage points and events.

"Like a prelude to death, an alternative awareness takes hold, diminishing the relevance of my body's host." It appears there is consciousness irrespective of the state of the body.

In times of quiet contemplation, I have posed rhetorical questions of my grandmother, and my father, who are now deceased. Yet, I always seem to know the answers. *"Does my grandmother know my son who was born many years after her death?"* The answer is "Yes." There appears to be answers to my Universe that I've always known the answers to. They do know each other, and also depend on each other.

"How my father would react in various situations."

I simply know, because I am living for him now. I feel his thoughts, his fears, and his reactions. I now understand why he used to wander off and get lost in crowds. Or how he would advise me to sell out of a business relationship, that in many ways echoed his own.

"There are relationships that transcend our place in time. These relationships are rooted in a common fork that direct our journey."

In the broader analysis, we are in a *"fragile aquarium,"* surrounded by a thin cage of air that we breathe. Limited and confined by our holding tank, our lives measure only a small part of our meaning here. We have found ways to pierce the container, but we're still trapped by our being, and taunted by what's gnawing on the other side.

As I reflect on such concepts in this book, I'd be the first to admit that my conclusions may not always be scientifically sound. I do acknowledge however, an absolute link between "science and reality," and someday we shall better confirm those links.

While we search for clues, and impose science for our verifications, there are undeniable powers of insight that we are born with. It's within these powers that I've extracted some of my greatest ideas, and also some of my greatest fears.

We live through history and adapt our essence from the past. Our insight is nothing more than a revelation within ones self. One day our science will connect the true nature of these realities, as we are on the cusp of some remarkable new insight.

"Nature is often hidden, sometimes revealed,
seldom extinguished"

—FRANCIS BACON

Much of what has been written here was conceived prior to my discovery of authors like, Karl Pribram, Michael Talbot, and Eben Alexander. To my surprise, many similar concepts have been described by others. The soul can be our best source of knowledge. Our internal conclusions can often be more revealing than standing on the shoulders of poets and other ideologues.

Some of my most powerful conclusions, center around the fact that, "reality" can take many forms and is often relative. We as humans create our own interpretations, and live in awareness that is independent of each other.

Further, we understand that time can be an illusion. Our identity is shaped by a multitude of influences both living and dead. Heaven is within us, not out there.., and our best answers often come from within.

Ideas are the germ of all matter. Without consciousness, matter would not exist at all. We are now discovering that thought is not generated from the brain as once believed. Instead, it acts as a conduit of energy that propels our reality. We are a combination of energy and focused consciousness, and that Universe is different for each one of us.

This book was written in response to a very special friend, whose faith in Christ has shaped his own destiny. He posed questions of me as to what I actually believed. After much reflection, I began to formulate concepts that spelled out my own personal belief system.

These ideas have evolved over time, and have brought me to a place of greater personal satisfaction. Connecting the soul is our most important mission in life. Through a range of methodologies, each one of us can shape our own valuable conclusions. Each living existence is most relative, and personal, and peers beyond space and time.

If you are easily offended by challenges to traditional religious perspective, **I recommend that you do not read this book!** My goal is to stretch traditional boundaries, and offer challenging insight as to what might be. I offer an infusion of ideas and perspectives that at the very least may solidify your own religious perspective.

The concepts in this book should stretch traditional versions of creation, and just might suggest new interpretations for how we perceive God.

Without trying to persuade a specific point of view, I shall walk through a belief system from a unique and most personal perspective. I hope you are inspired by this stimulating conversation. For this book, lays out the trail to my own personal heaven.

IN SEARCH OF THE HEAVENS

Part A

In Search of the Heavens

For centuries, we have looked to the heavens for strength and guidance from above. The mysteries of our Universe reveal a complex web of ideas and calculus that have formulated the reality of our world.

As far back as the early days of Mesopotamia, each city-state worshiped their own god. They worshiped a wide variety of deities and idols that influenced their daily activities. But, non so inspiring as in the ancient city of Babylon where Sumerians constructed the great Tower of Babel.

"It was a magnificent structure. It had rooms and rooms that touched the sky. Some called it the gateway to heaven." Inspired by the god Marduk, the tower rose higher and higher as to create its own entrance to paradise.

As it was told, God became angry with man because he worshiped other gods. He smashed this false temple into ruins, to separate heaven from earth. God discouraged man from thinking themselves as gods, and scrambled their language so they would not understand the wisdom of the skies. Heaven must remain a mystery, and man must remain a vigilant soldier in his adventures on earth.

Our first two Hebrew commandments outline, "thou shall have no other gods before me," and "thou shall not make graven images." For the rules were set in place for three major world religions.

Since the time our ancient ancestors first walked the earth, much history has passed. Our character has been shaped and guided by forces of curiosity and a quest for greater understanding.

We observe the sun moving across the sky, and watch a glowing moon at night. Certainly, we see order in this world, and a structure that overshadows humanity. Through the ages, we have speculated about the wonders of the Cosmos. *How big, how old, and how it all relates to our lives.*

While we try to unravel the mysteries of our existence, we have also empowered authorities to cement our past, and draft rules for our future. Our vision of the world has been shaped and conditioned slowly over the years.

We have adapted belief systems, from only a small cornerstone of knowledge. It's from these tiny particles of truth, that convictions are born, religion is sold, people die, and nations fall.

"We form islands of absolutes in an ocean of ever expanding knowledge. The problem is that absolutes are variable among our island, and the rocks are always shaken by widening horizons"

— M Z

As we reflect on our version of truth, let me make clear that no one holds the answers to the Universe. We see life from our own vantage. Our experience and up-bringing, our primal instincts, all contribute to an individual belief system. Like relativity in time and motion, *"Life,"* is relative on each plane of existence and from the vantage of the operator. We shall later explore those other vantages of reality.

Over the years, we have seen 10,000 variations of religion. Each one claims to hold the magic key to the vast unknowns. Each one creates its own symbolism, structures, and biases.

To gain favor in each community, one mirrors the strongest and loudest voices, and reinforces its concepts with absolute language. *"For them, the language of truth is the only way to gain entrance to heaven."* We have become the gatekeepers of our Universe.

We allow authorities to judge our ultimate value as human beings. Value in society is often based on religious conviction, and adherence to standards set forth by the community. Sadly, we have littered wreckage along the way. We have oppressed people of all faiths and divisions. Our history has been muddled in competing interests, as we are often the clay of other motivations.

People around the world have experienced retaliation for non-compliance. Conformity has been used as a strong tool of society, and thus cooperation is the key for ongoing survival.

When I was young, I used to listen to absolutes that were communicated through our congregation. There seemed to be a fundamental need for coherence. Later I came to realize, that most elders were simply conditioned over time, and had very few answers of their own. Life is indefinable, and thus our world is mostly ruled by faith. We all seem to rally around objective truths, and that consistency gives us our sense of comfort.

Our Journey

God is often described as a thinking and deterministic force throughout all of nature. That definition alone is restrictive and diminishes a wider interpretation. It doesn't allow for variations in purpose, or a more flexible relationship with the Universe.

As we journey through time and space, "God" may actually be better described as a process rather than a being. We are always on a journey for greater understanding. Our migration takes us through a natural transition. Humans are a part of God. "A piece of the multiplex!" This force is neither manipulative nor reverent. The great magnitude of God defies human interpretation, and most certainly all of its metaphors.

The vastness of our Universe demands wider thinking and greater accountability. We are ascended beings, trapped in this place and time. Our Universe is this box we call reality, and the true mission may actually be to evolve. The human challenge may best describe a "soulful evolution in search of the creator."

Along our journey, we struggle to find meaning in our existence. While we flirt with concepts, our rules guide us along the way. However, life affects our perceptions. We construct a world around a current vision. Survival mandates certain realities and also ongoing re-construction.

Every day we develop fresh interpretations of the world around us. We utilize our experience to form imagination and fresh concepts. Our storyline continues through our dreams at night, and our drama by day. Reality is often what we make it.

We've seen the creator taking many forms, and answering many different questions. The fact that we are human, offers enormous flexibility in thinking. We have created great civilizations and compiled long and lasting legacies. We have also created common formulas to define our righteousness.

These concepts have morphed into the central conscience of the human race. We adjust our logic to produce language that best fits our understanding. We have a hand in shaping this world.

Over the years, communities have formed alliances that may, *or* may *not* necessarily be divinely inspired. Most have ruled with their own brand of ideology for centuries.

As we accept rules of society, we should also consider rules in nature that also affect our experience. "Evolution" appears to be the ordered blueprint of all living and spiritual things. It is necessary to grow and flourish, and to master the wonders of the Universe. This best seems to fulfill God's will.

As we struggle to separate ideas from our own experiences, the world spins in a multitude of independent realities. We have little ability to judge this process, or its overarching divine purpose. To promote otherwise, would suggest human intervention.

Religion has promoted a means to bring greater understanding to our lives. Theologians have carved a world with explanations they can believe. The Torah, Bible, and Koran, all serve to fill these needs.

The concept of *"right and wrong," "heaven and hell," including "religion,"* is perpetuated by society to bring order. That order also happens to fulfill the prime directive given through our evolutionary process. *"Our rules give us our survival."*

We all have specific "blueprints" inherent within us! Humans must eat, sleep, flourish, and survive as a species. All earthly creatures appear to have similar ordered realities. Perhaps it is "we" that should be held to a higher standard due to our impact on the planet. However, that's a topic for another time.

Each species has a slightly different *"blueprint"* and unique *"responsibility,"* as does also the individual. Based on varied abilities, limitations, and biological uniqueness; the *"true will of God"* may be uniquely altered to fit the individual. Each person, animal, plant, or thing, has its own relationship with the Universe. Each follows a unique course through the cosmos. The concept of right or wrong is always subjective!

While we have discussed how civil rules support our survival, we also benefit from this structure. This further supports our prime directive. It is ordered that we live, experience, and evolve. Fulfillment of life, all its dreams, and a broader experience, will stretch our vantage and our access. We are in harmony with nature.

Those in defiance of societal rules will slow their migration.

An Individual becomes lost in direction and denied broader growth. This restricts the scope of life, or any grander opportunities. *"The individual becomes stagnant."*

It has been said that; *"hell is best defined as the absence of God."* I would further suggest that *"hell"* is the absence of growth and/or a confined state of reality.

The human challenge is to expand the possibilities, nurture the soul, and absorb greater perspective. Anti-social behavior will compromise our ability to survive and grow as an entity, and as a species.

"We live in both
Heaven and Hell"

Finding Perspective

Perspective is relative from human to human, species to species, aware-ness to awareness. Of the millions of living possibilities, as we know it, there are conscious possibilities of the *"non-living"* as well.

There are forms of awareness that we don't detect, or simply can't inter-pret. There are likely multi-dimensional levels of consciousness among organisms, time, matter, and intra-physical space. There are evolution-ary chains of energy that are currently beyond our level of recognition.

Consciousness takes on many forms. A plant can be aware of its own root system, and the correct amount of photosynthesis required. We as humans would be considered unplugged, unaware, and unconscious. There is intelligence in water that follows its own chemical path. A block of wood holds stored memory from its cellular origin as a tree. *(After all, its entire DNA code never changes.)*

When we die we also seem to have a relationship back to our original structure. ***"A block of wood may not know its dead!"***

Humans appear to possess knowledge beyond their physical presence. It remains clear that innate abilities and instincts were passed down from awareness outside of the human condition. When we die, we likely pass this awareness to other levels of consciousness.

To appreciate the vast multitude of universal realities, we must look beyond *"earthly"* self-serving terms, and realize grander evolutionary possibilities. We must recognize the broader perspective of what surrounds us.

"Ants and dogs don't comprehend Algebra!" We as humans can't even communicate effectively among species within our own environment, let alone with other vast subjective life forms.

In many ways, our senses are far too limited. We can't begin to comprehend the sight, sound, smell, or radar of a bottle nosed dolphin. With all our advancement, we have little ability to communicate with other species in our own environment.

Dolphins have agendas within their own Universe. Animals also possess their own sense of "right and wrong".

Dolphins have demonstrated temperaments and drive their young. They too must survive. They must evolve!

Attacking Dogs

A film recently showed a pack of wild dogs attacking a large snake. They attacked from all directions as the snake also struck back in all directions. The snake never got a hold of the dogs because they were too fast dodging the strike.

The question is, if the dogs had never been bitten before by the snake, how did the dogs know to dodge the head? What mechanism informed the dogs to avoid the head at all costs. How was the information transferred to the dogs?

In another example, a fly lands on my window seal. I swat and swat, but the damn fly is too fast! It seems to know when I am coming, and from what direction. It taunts me and laughs at my fully engaged attempts. I am worn out, and the fly flies on. How does it know that I want to kill it? Who taught the fly?

The fundamental question in behavior is our ability to understand danger or not, or gain "naturalistic instincts" as opposed to learned behaviors.

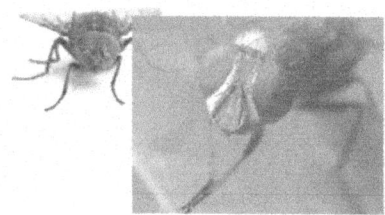

Perhaps the evolutionary process doesn't quite explain everything we see?

Instincts are not learned behaviors. They are natural tendencies coded within our DNA. Why birds fly south, or a salmon swims upstream? Why a fly evades motion? All somehow encoded in the DNA.

Birds in Flight

Is there a chemical coding that affects behavior? Or is it possible that such stimulus is a form of electrical energy.

Perhaps a type of transmitted voice from elsewhere.

One could make the argument that its not the DNA that is encoded at all, but rather a projection of presence. This would suggest a type of mirrored existence that we will explore later. If we solve the mystery of our instincts, we might well solve the mystery of the hand of God.

If we consider the "probability of chance," that instincts and biological forms were created by random selection alone, the math seems most insurmountable.

Dr. Robert Lanza, chief medical officer at Astellas Institute, Massachusetts, describes an amusing example of natural selection solely by mutation.

"If a million monkeys type on a million typewriters for a million years, you should get all the great works of literature. But here is the mathematical probability of creating just the first 15 characters of Moby Dick, "Call me Ishmael."

"There are 58 possible keys, and lets say that each monkey, types 45 words per minute. Now we have a million monkeys working day and night and never take a break or sleep. How long would it take for one of them to type, "Call me Ishmael"?

It would take 283 trillion, trillion attempts, and take 36 trillion years. This would be 1,000 times more than the age of the Universe. And there are exponentially more factors that would need to happen just to produce life as we know it."

Can we get the cosmos that we see, with all the complicated biological designs and brain power, through random collision of atoms alone? This suggests the role of consciousness may provide a better explanation for what we see, rather than the pure mathematics of natural selection.

If it takes thousands of years to simply, change the pigment of our skin, then it must take thousands upon thousands of eons, for natural selection to sort out survival tendencies and define protective instincts coded in our DNA. Through billions of trials, **it seems implausible to produce this degree of specialized mutation!**

Something more seems to be going on in the background.

Its that instinctual *feeling*, that 95% of the world population craves religion and a concept of an overseeing God.

In all likelihood, it's more about alternative methodologies in time and space, than about pure evolutionary processes. Somehow, we have experienced before. Knowledge is transferred and that process is the mystery of how we grow and think as a species.

An ongoing relation exists between matter and energy, and how it affects our being. Science has demonstrated over and over again the transferability of this fundamental relationship.

"If you want to find the secrets of the Universe, think in terms of energy, frequency and vibration."

— NIKOLA TESLA

Like so many questions in science, like the fact there is not enough matter in the Universe to hold stars and galaxies together.., so we conclude there *"must"* be dark matter! Holes need to be filled. Something more appears to be behind the scenes… and often we call it **God.**

God expresses our ultimate desires and patches the landscape of the vast unknowns. Basic principals in our science demonstrate a need to survive. We morph our biology as well as our instinctual spirit. And that ongoing spirit supports our path through the cosmos and guides us on through eternity.

Final Judgment

In the final judgment, there is probably no judgment at all. Just a movement through the process! All things in the Universe are in motion, and moving through an evolutionary trail to greater understanding. *"It is ordered!"*

Evil, hate, revenge, and wrath are human emotions. *"Not likely the emotions of an all encompassing God!"* *Therefore, forgiveness is irrelevant.* Only by nurturing and expanding our awareness, can we perpetuate the desired progression.

Humans have specific biological and social requirements inherent within us for survival. We must trust and follow the natural systems we've been handed. To do otherwise, alters our progression to God, and our right to existence!

TRAPPINGS OF TRADITION

Each of us holds a sacred responsibility to seek their own connection with the Universe. The primary purpose of the soul is to follow its own migration to truth! Therefore, those requiring a structured formula may gain a level of comfort *and/or* security, but may often fail to make an authentic connection!

Growth is not about following a system or being led down a path of tradition. It should be more about building on faith and personal connection, shaping destiny for the soul, and developing an individualized bridge through millennium.

In many ways, religion can be an obstacle to spiritual growth. Most confounding, are games and segregation that are often created, encouraging a world divided and in opposition with itself.

Truth seekers pour through volumes of doctrine and pronounce truth in the face of multiple realities. For the sake of tradition, so-called scholars recite what once *"inspired,"* while never accepting the fact that tradition and values constantly change over time, and evolve through spiritual rebirth.

Customs can also serve to alienate people. They encourage a kind of *"social club"* indoctrination. While it bonds a select group, it can also alienate those who are different. *(Unique language, jargon, and customs can also contribute to this kind of separation.)*

Those who wish to take part are usually welcome, regardless whether certain traditions have individual relevance or not! *"Come join in my culture but leave yours at the door!"* Similarly, those introducing contrary customs are perceived as threats to their own liberties and freedoms.

> **"Many who scream the loudest about infringement of religious freedoms, are often those who perpetuate their own separation, uniqueness and isolation."**
>
> **—MZ**

Adaptability is an important part of survival. Those who conform will generally enjoy support from others. Those outside of prevailing attitudes will often be ostracized.

A kind of arrogance enters the theatre as those with "absolute knowledge" impose beliefs on the rest of the world. This has proven over many centuries to lead to conflict.

From an outside perspective, the trappings of tradition can be an extraneous, combative, and wasteful use of energy, without necessarily contributing to spiritual growth.

"It can be like watching endless games of tick- tack- toe, a child stacking cubes, or drawing stick figures against a three dimensional sky"......

—M Z

There have been many examples where I have celebrated a family gathering or religious event. Due to the solemn nature of the ceremony, I was held captive for several hours while various religious competitors demonstrated how well versed one could recite the poetry. It became a kind of competition in an effort to prove who was the most religious.

Conversation usually revolved around the church and/or synagogue, and may have sacrificed the rare opportunity to converse with extended family. Unfortunately, due to time limitations and busy lifestyles, we never actually had the chance to converse or learn much about each other's lives.

When churches fall into this trap, it creates a self-affirming and restrictive value system that locks itself into a particular brand of methodology and sub-culture.

For example, when deciding what songs to sing in worship, they usually return to songs that have been formative or meaningful and repeat them. This perpetuates the tradition, and promotes a particular culture and era.

Often clergy will devote a large percentage of their practice toward ritualistic customs rather than family counseling or daily practical guidance.

Families typically go through regular struggles and need to rely on strength from a supportive and therapeutic clergy. It would seem to be an important and often neglected special role, that all too many overlook in the wake of due process.

Growing up in the 60s, there was a lot of discussion about norms and standards in society. Their was a proper way to dress, eat, and act. Tradition was simply expected.

Alarm bells went off when there were suddenly new movies, arts, and music. Rock 'n' roll was once considered by some to be the music of the Devil. The whole anti-war culture including long hair and casual dress became the objection of the established community.

"Civil disobedience is not our problem. Our problem is that people are obedient all over the world in the face of poverty, starvation, stupidity, war, and cruelty."

—HOWARD ZINN

"Religion is what keeps the poor from murdering the rich."

—NAPOLEON

"Imagine there's no heaven. It's easy if you try. No hell below us, above us only sky. Imagine all the people living for today."

—JOHN LENNON

I remember when a young progressive Sunday school teacher brought a guitar and restructured traditional worship songs. While the elders in the congregation looked with puzzlement, the kids all seemed to connect in this new time and experience.

Sacrifice

It was an established custom within many religions and cults, where the act of killing or *"sacrifice,"* was a necessary offering in order to renew life. Victims were typically ritually killed in a manner that was supposed to please or appease gods, spirits, or the deceased.

According to the Book of Genesis, God commands Abraham to offer his son Isaac as a sacrifice. After Isaac was bound to an altar, God stops Abraham at the last minute, saying, "now I know you fear God." Abraham looks up, sees a ram, and sacrifices it instead of Isaac.

Human sacrifice has been practiced in various cultures throughout history. Over time, these ritualistic practices became less common, however, are still valued and symbolized in our modern religious practices.

During the Crusades, Christians vilified Jews in a bid to gain more converts. They accused Jews of outlandish acts such as "blood libel" - the kidnapping and murder of Christian children to use their blood to make Passover bread. Blood libel was used to describe the most heinous of old-world Jewish customs by non-other than Adolph Hitler as a tool of propaganda and persecution.

Today, we symbolize the drinking of bread and wine to be the consumption of Christ. We translate these ancient traditions and devote a considerable amount of our energy in replicating these religious practices.

Kosher laws as demonstrated by the Jewish religion were originally designed to test man's obedience with God. While there is practical hygienic value in these dietary customs, many practices defy the advent of the FDA and modern scientific understanding.

The Mennonites continue to practice a generally simple and unsophisticated life. Many have chosen to live free of electricity and modern conveniences, such as television and automobiles. Hardship seems to be an intrinsic value in ones allegiance to God.

The Renaissance period moved us from a time when we believed the world to be flat, and the Earth was the spiritual center of the Universe. The purpose of science in the middle ages was to gain a better understanding of God, not the workings of the world. Any medieval scientist would have found it inconceivable to examine the Universe outside the realm of religion.

It was the likes of Copernicus, Galileo, and Newton, that introduced new science based on natural laws, and not the workings of a mysterious God. Many rituals began to move slowly toward symbolism, rather than in actual practice. However, we continue to hold great reverence over these ancient concepts.

Today, the roots of our religious practices are based from origins in primitive customs and rituals. Within today's modern society, we still subject ourselves to a considerable fixation with these ancient customs.

Theologians through history have defined absolutes such as, anti-racial relationships, traditional women's rights, and customary religious perspective, while often failing to recognize new sets of evolving principals.

Religion has often spun itself into knots trying to rationalize traditional values, while morphing its message in a maze of ambiguity. Culture changes, and our ideals continue to evolve.

In the past, we have seen religious doctrine used as a weapon for a host of ulterior motives. Generally speaking, the church has exercised unchallenged control and authority throughout history. Its domination has been most absolute.

Some of its disciples have even produced antagonists willing to cast others into the fires of damnation.

Through the ebb and flow of social justice, we have established common rules as our vehicle to get to heaven. However, the value of self-awareness may better serve our spiritual growth. *"We are on a daily mission for truth,"* and our world holds a vast array of answers. Those who practice self-discovered enlightenment may actually find greater power and comfort. Many times the best answers are from within.

"It's hard to see how a flock of sheep will find the holy land." —MZ

My Temple

Each of us seeks to find spiritual identity in our own way.

The opportunity to get in touch with spirit is paramount for the nourishment of the soul. To feel free, alive, and creative seems to best fulfill our natural directive.

"Meditating in nature, a quiet car ride, to focus on music, creativity, or to push the body to maximum endurance, instills feelings of value and fulfillment. One can certainly tap a connection with the soul."

We interact with God in many ways. God is visible everywhere and in many forms. He represents freedom and opportunity, unlike the chaining to a temple or cathedral. We have a need to pray, and that solitude whether by cathedral or nature, can revitalize the spirit and energize the soul. God is a strong case in flexibility.

Many wrap themselves in a *"religious security blanket"* for a whole host of reasons. A religious affiliation can represent an identifiable and exclusive membership! Many find comfort in traditions and repetition of the familiar.

To sit in front of *"dogmatic ritualistic processes"* can have a stifling effect! The soul is filtered and original inspiration suppressed, as one mumbles jargon of religious procedure. Reciting scripture becomes the focus over thought and deed. *"Often a practice of rhetoric over positive action."*

However, churches and places of worship can also provide great testaments for historic values. These structures are symbols for the community and provide "strength" in the face of a chaotic world.

The Cherokee utilize all of nature as their house of worship. To experience the right of passage, a young boy is led into the forest with a blindfold and left alone to meet with God.

> *"He is required to sit on a stump the whole night and not remove his blindfold until the morning sun. He cannot cry out for help to anyone. The wind blows the grass and earth and shakes his stump, but he must sit stoically never uncovering his eyes.*
>
> *Finally, after a horrific night, the sun appears and he can remove his blindfold. He is now a Man. He finds his father sitting beside him. Even when we aren't aware, he learns that God is watching over, and always protecting us."*

Native American culture is known for its rich oral traditions. Instead of written language to document history, they rely on storytelling to share customs, rituals, and legends through vivid narratives.

These powerful tales, often told by tribal elders to younger generations, both entertain and preserve tribal heritage. Each time a story was told, it breathes new life into the culture. Lessons are taught concerning love, leadership, and honor, as well as a symbiotic relationship with the earth and nature.

As a way to heighten senses and encourage a deeper connection with the environment, stories told, are often accompanied with song, music, and dance. Native Americans celebrated rituals before and after hunting expeditions. Spirituality drives on-going success.

Many native tribes have leaders called Shamans. Spirits enter a Shaman's body during the ceremonies, and by beating drums and chanting, the ceremony is more inspirational.

A willow hoop, called a dream catcher is often hung over the bed as protection. It serves to engulf the area and prevent evil spirits from entering their prescribed temple or residence.

The Hoppe Indians designate sacred lands as a means of entrapping great spirits. It's from ones dreams that spiritual identity emerges. These lands hold special significance.

In another story, a holy man would shout into the blackness of a cave. If he hears his echo, he knows it is reflected back from God. With a closed entrance, one can catch dreams and re-live new spiritual identity.

Historically, tribal leaders who practiced Native American spirituality were sometimes subjected to a jail term of thirty years. The U.S. and Canadian governments forcibly tried to change the way Native Americans practiced, by converting them to their so-called suitable religions.

In the grand scheme of things, one who satisfies personal convictions and expands the scope of their life should find authentic spiritual growth. Man adapts to his environment and creates his own spirituality.

Whatever means or methodology, an *"inspired"* existence maximizes our living experience, and guides us through an evolutionary trail to better *"understanding."*

A fulfilled existence nurtures the natural process. Our consciousness as human beings becomes rewarded. The soul finds renewed energy in its ongoing experience.

We may yet find our heaven.........

Finding Religion

Religion launched the science of its day. It exemplified the latest in thinking while forwarding early hypotheses of the world and creation. It bonded society, developed norms, and standards while comforting emotional needs. Any enlightened member of society would learn and study its example. *"For these were the true scholars and teachers."*

Religion was promoted as a means for humans to adapt a connection with God. The reality is there are many roads to God and each person must make their own vehicle.

As discussed earlier, finding God is the process of fulfillment of life, expanding horizons, and establishing standards to live by that best support evolutionary growth. *(Not necessarily the practice of ritualistic customs.)*

Many of our customs share an eerie resemblance to those who worshiped idols before us. And many of those ancient pagan practices became the catalyst for our modern systems of worship.

THE MINDS OF THE GODS

From Mount Olympus, the gods fired lightning bolts from the sky…
And as the thunder rumbled across the city states of Greece in 500 BC,
the people trembled in submission.

For Zeus held the power of life and death over their world.

Twelve Gods carried out specific tasks from the heavens as they ruled
all aspects of their Life. The people worshiped their "greatness," and
glorified their presence with constellations all over the night sky.

It was said that Zeus created the present race of humans. Several
races existed before, but Zeus eliminated them when it no longer

suited his needs. Zeus would likely destroy the current race should he become displeased.

Ruling from paradise far above the clouds where only gods could reach, these *"Olympians"* conferred together making decisions on the fate of mortals, as they feasted on ambrosia and sipped wine.

The Gods interacted with man in many ways, often sharing their offspring, dialogue, and inspiration. Above all, they ruled over the heavens… and demanded absolute obedience.

> *"Apollo drug the sun across the sky, as he lit a trail of light for the world below. His four-horse chariot danced in the sky as he pronounced prophecy for what was yet to come"*

> *"Ares shook the earth with mighty quakes so violent it would wake his enemies. War was a necessary part of the heavens and man must be a vigilant soldier to survive in this world. The weak will parish from the earth!"*

> *"Poseidon pitched great waves in the sea straddled by his army of serpents. Seamen gave worship to his powerful authority. Poseidon was one of three super-gods that divided all of creation"*

> *Zeus ruled the sky, Hades controlled the underworld, and Poseidon was master of the "grand seas"*

These were just a few of the great and powerful gods that ruled over the ancient world. The temperaments of the gods were a regular cycle of life. Man lived in fear of the heavens, and paid tribute with great temples and places of worship.

During this age, many scholars wrestled with questions concerning the origins of the world. In direct conflict with Greek mythology, both had their influence on current religions.

Great Philosophers

Socrates   Plato   Aristotle

By the 4th century BC, Greek philosophers like Socrates, Plato, and Aristotle, lived in a world mostly influenced by mythological views. These philosophers promoted ideas that threatened standards of their time. Accused of *"heresy"* and *"atheism,"* they challenged authority and conventional wisdom of God and the heavens.

They probed fundamental ideas such as the essence of *"substance."* It was believed that "Fire," "Earth," "Air," and "Water" ruled the makeup of everything in the Universe. Aristotle also included *"Ether,"* as the Devine spiritual substance that made the intangibles of life. They raised new questions of reality, both physically and spiritually.

In medieval days, Augustine and Aquinas introduced controversial ideas that eventually became the bedrock of many churches today. In the late 1600s, Isaac Newton introduced *"fundamental laws of nature,"* which further complicated the accepted standards of his time.

Galileo, when searching the skies, also expressed ideas contrary to the church. He suggested that the earth actually revolves around the sun, not the other way around. As with all threats to established religion, free-thinkers challenged prevailing attitudes and threatened authority.

"I do not believe the same God who endowed us with sense, reason, and intellect, intended us to forgo its use."

—GALILEO

Often in conflict with the current dogma, these ideas pushed the envelope of humanities, and dared to look at life outside the conventional box. This was often met with great sacrifice.

In all eras, contrary world views have led to persecution and hardship, often discouraging broader thinking about the world.

Even today.., we recognize the challenge that unique ideas bring to prevailing attitudes. This continues to be the test of *"free speech"* in a society dominated by a specific brand of political correctness.

Writing this book has posed its own challenges & discretion as to whom should even see it! Today, it is most unwise to oppose traditional religious values, tax the church, or weed out hypocrisy when presented next to science.

Our moral system established by religion, has at times been pushed by practical applications of growth and logic. And these influences have given our world its own battle of the gods.

Throughout history, paganism exemplified a range of tradition that often related to the cycles of the earth. With an ongoing presence in nature, it has been widely accepted that strong forces in the background are ruling our world.

In the land of Canaan, the powerful god, "El" was worshiped by Abraham, and became the original god of the Jewish people. That same God has changed and evolved over time, inciting new and ever changing meaning.

The idea that *"souls go to heaven after death"* originated in the very earliest of pagan beliefs in Babylon and Egypt. These early concepts arrived long before the Greeks, or even the Israelites.

As early as 5500 B.C., people of Northeast Africa worshiped ancient Egyptian gods as protectors, guides, and ultimate supreme beings. Their myths describe everything from creation to afterlife, including the eternal soul of man.

As we practice our current religions, we have borrowed from these same concepts. Many practices have stemmed from the myths of our past. In so many ways *"Osiris lives!"*

THE CYCLE OF LIFE

The Ancient Egyptians best exemplified the concept of life after death. They believed in the incarnation of spirit in the form of five key Gods.

Osiris represents the divine immortal soul. *Ra* is the light of consciousness. *Isis,* rules all of time and eternity. *Horus* is the individuality of each human soul. And *Thoth* rules all of human intellect.

These Gods unite the universe with connected gateways to the spirit world. Reincarnation can link man's existence in future lives, and grant opportunity for eventual liberation of the soul.

King Tutankhamen in 1343 B.C., wrapped in shrouds and entombed in a private vault. His body is sealed for life ever after!

Death is simply a temporary interruption, and not the cessation of life. Eternity is ensured through mummification and a devoted worship of the gods. Art is displayed to preserve the eternal story.

"When the gods formed the land out of chaos, "Maat" was anointed to personify the perfect order." It was through the ideals of this great goddess, that Egyptians were allowed entrance into the next world.

Afterlife is achieved by preserving the body in mummification, and honoring prescribed arts and writings on the tomb walls. The spirit world is enhanced through all of eternity.

Hindu Similarities

The ancient Hindus practiced a very similar philosophy in the Indus River Valley as far back as 1000 B.C.

The mission of life is to also serve the lofty ideals of the Gods.

By doing so, one can join the creator in eventual afterlife. Enlightenment is achieved through cycles of birth and death known as "Samsara." Cycles and regular evolution are an ongoing theme of the Hindu religion.

The accumulation of all one's good and bad deeds determine the next incarnation. The caste one is born into is influenced by the previous life.

The soul reincarnates again and again and reunites with its maker. The soul enters many bodies, assumes many forms, and passes through many birth and death cycles. This is described in the *Bhagavad-Gita*.

*"Like worn out clothes, the soul discards worn out
bodies and assumes new ones."*

—BG 2.22

The great cycle of rebirth stretches over millions of years. After each life cycle, the body returns to earth and assumes new life. The *"Jiva"* and *"Soul"* however, survive death and wonder on throughout eternity.

Hiding in the spirits core, the *"Jiva"* remains in this world, until it exhausts results of good and bad behaviors. Having learned, it returns to earth again to take another birth.

Ancient views such as the *"Egyptians,"* *"Hindus,"* and also the *"American Indians,"* are consistent with spiritual evolution, and the attainment of God through various planes of reality. Not by the concept of finite birth and death as believed in the west.

Western philosophy was introduced by the Roman Empire in the 4th Century A.D., as Christianity spread throughout all of Europe. Eventually, it was brought to the Americas.

Western civilization views life in a more linear and final progression. After creation, man experiences life on earth and then "final judgment." Right and wrong is laid out in biblical formula and determines the final restitution of the soul.

Christianity teaches God created each person as part of a master plan. One's lifetime is an ongoing trial of sins and judgments for all eternity.

Christians refer to the *"sanctity of life"* when considering issues of "abortion," "euthanasia," "embryo research," or the care of the disabled or the elderly. To deliberately end a life, even one of a terminally ill patient, is destroying a life that God has created.

"Before I formed you in the womb, I knew you before you were born"

—JEREMIAH 1:5

Judaism teaches that all life is granted from one God as well.

Jews also believe that man is destined for judgment in either heaven or hell. The difference is that the messianic age has not yet come to deliver man to his eventual eternal outcome. "Heaven is waiting," and the savior, has not yet come.

Since God created life, only he is permitted to decide when a person should die. Euthanasia and suicide are against the teachings of Jewish scripture and the Torah.

"Only God holds responsibility over Life and Death"

—GENESIS 28:3

"Thou shalt not Kill"
—Gods 6th Commandment.

Traditional Judaism is opposed to life altering acts, however Jewish scripture is also used to argue that people should not be kept on life-support when there is little hope of recovery.

The Talmud reflects discussions among ancient rabbis on Jewish law, ethics, customs, and practices. It describes early oral traditions and its historical commentary on life and death.

In all these examples.., the overriding theme is man's relationship with God and his own mortality. While no one endorses the killing of life, each culture places a particular importance on preparation for the hereafter.

The spirit holds a special place in the human condition. And that spirit even overshadows the value of life in importance.

In all cases, judgments of life and death are elevated to the eventuality of the soul. ***"Death of body is not death of spirit."***

To Live or Die

In viewing the concept of life and death, certain key considerations might shape our values and under-standing of the process.

When a conscious decision is made to end a life through *"Abortion," "Capitol punishment," "Eutha-nasia," or "Suicide,"* These actions could be rationalized for one of the following reasons.

Either;

A. The *"progression"* of a specific life form has a severely restricted opportunity to grow and develop within its current existence, *(Jailed, handicapped, or sick)*

Or

B. Extreme *"suffering"* would limit the quality of life, thus not conducive for further spiritual growth and evolution.

Proponents of choice believe the quality of life can be more important than life itself. The giving of life is a natural process and would be granted again and again. The soul always continues. Life in some circumstances can actually be a hindrance to spiritual growth and soulful evolution.

It is easy to rationalize either of the previous two positions in association with common value systems. After all, religious wars and governments rationalize the taking of life for simple property and resources.

"We condition ourselves to believe we have a divine right to own property and resources, and to even to kill for it!"

One might justify the taking of life for reasons of *"suffering"*, or a *"limited opportunity"* to grow spiritually in ones journey toward the creator.

In the grand scheme of things, humans shouldn't be making these judgments at all. *And that includes governments!*

However, the taking of life in general is part of survival in nature and *not* necessarily judged in the eyes of the cosmos. Its the taking of a developing life that becomes the tragedy, and is counter productive for the growth and survival of the species.

"It's not given to people to judge what's right or wrong. People have eternally been mistaken and will be mistaken in what they consider right and wrong."

—LEO TOLSTOY, WAR AND PEACE

"It is forbidden to kill; therefore all murderers are punished, unless they kill in large numbers and to the sound of trumpets."

—VOLTAIRE

When is it Alive?

On the discussion of "abortion" the debate centers around definition of life and what circumstances justifies this action.

As a human egg matures, its physical development becomes increasingly more significant over time. Early stages of nerves and sensory are not fully developed yet. Early cells resemble that of corn, grass, or bacteria. Yes, it holds the magic DNA blueprint.., but so does every piece of skin that falls off the body, or blood and urine lost.

During the earliest stages, an embryo is not yet considered a human. It is part of a natural biological process that has billions of false starts daily, and can be stimulated an unlimited number of times through biological interaction.

It is within our power to create from an unlimited supply of cells. *"There is nothing mystical about one egg over another, or even one fertilized egg over another."*

One, who accepts the concept of divine intervention, might assume an argument such as; *"It's God's will to preserve as many fertilized eggs as possible."* Thus, we would encourage a type of limitless baby factory.

It's that absurd notion that suggests, it is man by natural process, and the *"probability of chance,"* that manipulates fertilization. God is simply not responsible for each act. *"Only the ordered laws that govern each act."* This of course, continues to be the focus of much ongoing debate!

Abortion is a natural event in the movement of a traveling Universe. *"This event is likely insignificant in the master scope of the cosmos."* Creatures live and die, and they also become extinct.

"Souls are the force of life, and belong to God. Therefore, man has little influence over life or death of the soul." —MZ

DNA demonstrates that every cell in the body can be reproduced over and over again. Life is common and most abundant wherever carbon conditions for life are favorable. The more we learn about the human genome, the more we recognize the mechanical nature of the production of life.

The definition of life has been debated many times through the years. In 1821, Connecticut passed the first state statute criminalizing abortion. Every state had abortion legislation by 1900.

In the 1950s, Hospitals formed *"therapeutic abortion boards"* to decide when doctors could perform an abortion on a case-by-case basis. This created great inconsistencies of practice.

In 1973, the US Supreme Court ruled that women had a fundamental right to abortion under the United States Constitution. That right, however, would be balanced against state's restrictions after the third trimester.

The Court affirmed in the case of Roe versus Wade, that a person has a legal right to abortion until viability. Viability being defined as; *"able to live outside the mother's womb,"* usually placed at about the seventh month.

Abortion is as controversial abroad as it is in the United States. Many governments struggle to strike a balance between the rights of pregnant women and the rights of unborn fetuses.

The following are examples of current policy:

Great Britain Abortion is freely available in Great Britain due to the Abortion Act of 1967, which permits abortion for a variety of reasons if certified by two physicians.

Germany Although a 1995 law makes abortion illegal, neither doctors nor women are prosecuted if the procedure is performed within 12 weeks of conception.

Canada The Supreme Court of Canada in 1988 ruled that former abortion restrictions were unconstitutional. Abortion today is legal for any reason, however it is not State funded.

Russia reportedly leads the world in the total number of abortions performed each year, which currently exceeds the country's annual number of live births.

China Abortion is freely available in China and there are no defined time limits for the procedure. Although sex-selective abortion is prohibited, critics say that China's one-child-per-family policy encourages the widespread abortion of female fetuses.

Israel A 1977 law made abortion legal in Israel to save the mother's life or to preserve her mental or physical health. The Israeli Penal Law forbids causing the death of another, and specifically forbids shortening the life. Both Israeli and Jewish law forbids active euthanasia.

Japan's Eugenic Protection Law of 1948, promoted liberal policies on abortion and sterilization with the intent of fostering a genetically healthy population. In 1996, new legislation omitted all references to eugenics and established regulations making abortion legal within the first 24 weeks. Japan is the only country where voluntary euthanasia permitted.

In the United States, Abortion is legal on request and has allocated federal funds to do so. Euthanasia is illegal in most of the United States. Patients, however, retain the right to refuse medical treatment and to receive appropriate management of pain at their request.

Capital punishment also continues to be debated at the state level. Whether it is considered punishment, or in the greater interest of society, each state has determined its own course of action. A key consideration revolves around the cost of appeals and the lengthy process associated with discovery.

In western society, little consideration is given to the moral implications itself. In a secular society, we have often made determinations based on a wide range of special interests. And those special interests are often influenced by socio-economic factors as well as current political momentum.

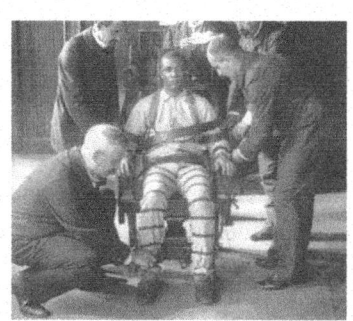

"Every State has a different point of view"

ONE HUNDRED GENERATIONS

"Our Trail from Abraham."

The trail from Abraham has greatly influenced our current genetic and cultural reality. We have borrowed from ancient societies and been influenced by the theologies that rule the world around us. We have created specific pools of genetics through our segregation, and have forged our own brand of social awareness.

Disease, illness, and physical attributes all resulted from common roots characterized by branches of our past. That is why humans fall into very specific *"haplo-groups"* as defined by genetic family migration patterns. Christians, Jews, and Muslims alike can all lay claim back to Abraham.

DNA code is rarely ever altered by mutation. It takes many years to slowly change. The footprints of our genetic past go back thousands of years, and match descendants from a rich and most common fork.

The amazing thing is, how our lineage has been so strongly preserved over the years, through strict cultural bonds and religious confinement.

Prior to Abraham, tribes migrated together and formed their own brand of ethnicity. Through our own practice, we have inadvertently encouraged separate genetic populations and distinctive family units.

The world is very small, and our lineage is very close. Our time frames are insignificant in viewing a relationship with a master God. A conversation about *Abraham,* or any other biblical ancestor for that matter, is more like a conversation about great grandparents. Our patriarchal roots back to Abraham, pose many common insights.

A generation of 30 years yields 80 (eighty) generations since the time of Abraham.

According to the Bible, prior to the great flood, men lived many hundreds of years. Adam lived 930, Seth, Enos, and Noah about 900 years each. After the flood, men lived only about 300 years up until Roman times.

Abraham was 130, and most of his offspring were over 100. Assuming the Bible is *"correct,"* and that mankind is roughly 6,000 years old, we should be able to extrapolate the total number of human generations.

Prior to the flood, men lived hundreds of years. After the time of Moses, life expectancy gradually decreased to what we know as 70 years today.

The Jewish people have seen about 80 generations since the inception of Judaism. Adam and Eve were created around 4,000 BC. *(2,000 years prior to Abraham)* Thus, the human race has seen only **"one hundred"** generations in its 6,000 year history.

25% increase per surviving generation, takes 30 generations to reach one million people.

Something Changed

Obviously, the same norms and standards do not apply today. Did God once have a different relationship from what we now share? Did men once live hundreds of years and regularly observe ongoing miracles?

Or, could events and accounts be a metaphoric translation. This would open the door for a *"figurative"* interpretation of the Bible.

Science relies on consistent rules of observation to project the future. In light of these strange generational intervals as outlined in the Bible, something changed over time. *"The same observations, no longer apply."*

If we accept *"order in the Universe"* and *"fundamental laws in nature,"* then the literal accounts described in the Bible must be challenged. The Bible as an accurate source from God should be questioned.

If we can't rely on consistencies in our Universe, we are destined for a life of chaos and unpredictability. This implies a state of vulnerability. ***"Above all we need our Gods to be predictable!"***

A third option is that *"it happened the way God said it did, but* his inter-actions have changed over time." This describes a God of changing laws and methodologies, and **not** a God of absolutes. This implies a changing or evolving force in nature. Changing laws in nature violate the very essence of truth.

Burning bush

My own personal ancestors accepted the *"Old Testament as the word of God,"* and built temples and communities around a reality they so believed.

If the spirit of Judah is imbedded in my soul, passed down from the roots of Abraham, then there have been only a limited number of generations since creation. Thus, God's hand is very finite indeed.

Projectable Science

The scientific method implies that current observations are projectable into the future. This describes a methodology of forecasting. We know from science, and all we hold as true, that there are consistent laws throughout nature.

Science always yields predictable outcomes. There has never been a single example authenticated by science, where the laws of nature change to produce supernatural outcomes. We have always found verifiable explanations.

While we have always heard claims of the *"walking dead"* or *"magical elves"*.., there has never been **one** example of provable evidence for such phenomena.

Humans have strong & vivid imaginations. We often have difficulty separating facts from our own fiction. Man creates a world of reality that often has nothing to do with the macro- Universe around him. This seems to be the state of our reality.

In grasping for answers to unsolved mysteries, we generate theories and versions based on emotion. We convince our- selves of a reality characterized by faith. *(Faith is belief, nothing more)*

Man instills values and principals in strangely similar depictions of his own terms and experiences. "Reward and punishment," "obedience," "controls on family," all dictates awareness perpetuated by our society.

Storytelling has been one of the greatest tools to engage communities with complex social issues. This can drive beliefs, and consolidate opinions. People are more likely to accept information if it reaches them in the form of a good story.

> **"The art of storytelling is most impactful, as our epic slice of truth and wisdom, is so ever elusive."**
>
> **—WALTER BENJAMIN**

> **"Sometimes reality is too complex. Stories give us resolution."**
>
> **– JEAN LUC GODDARD**

> **"Stories constitute the single most powerful weapon in a leader's arsenal."**
>
> **– HOWARD GARDNER**

Whether mandated by belief or not, leaders of nations build strength and control around enforcement of these ideals. **Those who don't consent, they can't control.** They often become enemies of the state. *(Jews have often fallen prey to such reactions)*

Today, we witness no direct interaction from God, other than purely subjective or emotional interpretations. This strongly suggests that we may be spinning our own reality. Certainly, our relationship with God is not as once described.

Science in Conflict

In the beginning, God created the heavens and the earth, and he commanded, *"Let there be light."* The sun, moon, and stars were not created until the 4th day. *What was the source of the light on that first day of creation?*

If Creation was 6,000 years ago, are we left to dismiss the science of carbon dating, or evidence that dinosaurs and other extinct creatures ever once existed?

"Do animals get to heaven if they have not yet accepted a savior? What about the mentally challenged, or the young that die early? Can one *"sometimes"* get to heaven without acceptance? That would also seem to be in conflict with the literal translation.

Why do we cling to beliefs with such passion when logic tells us something very different? Do we try to trick ourselves into a belief system?

There obviously is comfort in a system. But, as various belief systems conflict.., warring parties often become the result! We condition ourselves to take a stand and to die for it! This seems most counter-productive for our survival. History is littered with religious righteous-ness, as well as religious early graves.

Inevitable Conclusion

Man seeks answers to his Universe and invents religion.

That religion bonds a unique culture that encourages assimilation of standards. Ethnic uniqueness creates conflict with other alternative truth seekers. Man annihilates man and may never discover the true essence of our Universe.

Those who believe they know *"the truth"* may actually be the most dangerous to society. These so-called *"fanatics"* are generally uncom-promising, and share many traits with modern terrorist. They convince themselves of their own truth, justify their own actions, and make their own rules of engagement. Social order is maintained as long as their brand of truth is consistent with those dominating the society around them.

Evidential Creditability

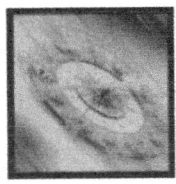

The first writing and written records were recorded about 900 B.C. Scientifically, evidence suggests life spans were closer to 40 years old rather than 300 as claimed in the Bible.

There is only a small percentage of the world's population that know anything at all about their grandparents, let alone *"great"* grandparents. *"Generations get lost in a shroud."*

Today, with all the advantages of longer and overlapping life spans, better written records, and general communications, we still don't know much about our grandparents just a few generations up the tree…

How would one begin to judge the creditability of passed down information from hundreds-of-years ago, while relying on records that were far more haphazard?

The most fundamental information concerning our oldest known relatives is often sketchy at best. What town did they come from? When did they immigrate, and under what circumstances? How did they meet? What were their religious convictions?

"I would venture to say that 90% of Americans do not know this most basic information, just 3 generations removed."

Most pre-civilized people were extremely nomadic! How do you suppose they communicated their family histories?

The disciples recognized Jesus after his death, *"not of flesh, but of spirit."* The events were written in the New Testament *Book of Revelations,* more than 200 years after the death of Jesus.

There was a 1,950-year time span between Adam and Abraham. *(Abraham must have had some amazing records...)*

This equates to me reciting the events of Rollo, and the Viking invasion of 950 AD.. Somehow, Abraham's lineage managed to record generations prior to written history, and captured the essence of events and early conversations with God.

Propagation of the Species

"God spoke to Noah and commanded him to build a great Ark. He should round up two of each kind to spare them from a world of wickedness."

According to Genesis, Noah brought his wife and three sons *(Shem, Ham, and Japheth)* along with their wives. The Book of Tobit describes Noah's wife as a relative. The Book of Jubilees identified Noah's wife as *Emzara* daughter of Rake'l, son of Methuselah. Their son's wives "Sedeqetelbab",

"Ne'elatama" and "Adataneses" were also children of Noah and Emzara.

In three places in the Torah, it codifies family members of which sexual relationships are prohibited. In Leviticus, marriages are strictly forbidden between parent and child, between siblings and up to third cousins.

We know that children with close biological relationships have an increased risk of congenital disorders, death, and genetic abnormalities caused through inbreeding.

As Noah loaded the animals two by two, he propagated incestuous relationships as siblings mated with each other to propagate the species. This, being in direct violation of recognized biblical law. *Perhaps God made an exception.*

God and the Ten Commandments

The bible describes how Moses received 10 commandments from God and it was written down on two tablets. Every image presented in Sunday school or anywhere else for that matter, shows the tablets written in Hebrew. Moses and the tablets are described in Exodus as being received from God at Mount Sinai with an approximate biblical date of 1265BC.

The problem is that Hebrew writing did not exist until around 700BC. The earliest known alphabet of Phoenician origins emerged around 900BC. Therefore, the commandments were written more than 300 years prior to any known written alphabet. That would make inscribing language into stone very difficult.

Since an Egyptian Princess raised Moses, he likely would have been Egyptian. There are no depictions of Egyptian Hieroglyphics anywhere related to the commandments, and it would be most difficult to describe these laws in a pictorial format.

When the Israelites continued to worship golden calves, Moses smashed the tablets into a million pieces. God then re-transcribed the commandments once again for his people that could not have read them anyway.

"Now that's a great Communicator!"

Other Biblical Details

Since the earth was in existence on the 1st day of creation, without form and void, it appears that the earth was created before the sun, moon, stars, and other planets…

"So much for the big bang theory!"

On the 2nd day of creation, God commanded let it rain, *but in day 1, God already was hovering over the face of the waters.*

On the 4th day, God said "Let there be lights in the heaven to divide day and night." *So apparently, the earth was created before the stars in the sky. I guess the sun was something different than the stars.*

On the 6th day, God created man in his image in the Garden of Eden. God warned not to eat from the tree of knowledge that contained both good and evil. *So, in other words, "knowledge is bad."*

On the 7th day, God became tired and rested! *So, if God becomes tired, he must also be vulnerable.*

We have gained a great deal of character and personality from these ancient concepts. As a civilization, we have often stretched the bounds of logic with comfortable concepts and explanations of the world around us. The story of God is an ever-changing process, and our stories always migrate to fit the occasion.

Abraham is the father of three great world religions, the genetic compass of our soul, and the designer of our cultural heritage. He has laid out a trail from our creator. Accurate or not, it has become our spiritual destiny.

REALITY
IS RELATIVE

Part B

Social Reality

Human beings have established some remarkable beliefs through the years. We have clung to valuable traditions, and hold a unique bird's eye view of the world that surrounds us.

Historically, the biblical version of our world has been the established dogma that ensured our survival. All opposed would be sentenced to a life of separation and disadvantage within society.

Over time, a conditioning took place where people lived under the dominant shadow of the church. The powerful hand of the clergy homogenized every thought and deed. Community watchdogs helped ensure this chosen behavior.

Daily activity was often regimented by time of day, language of choice, acceptance of standards, and enforced obedience as necessary for survival. Methodologies were established to ensure dominance within this unique cast system.

Beyond just this theology, there was a need for a defined food chain. This food chain has been predicated by systems that maintain ongoing advantage.

As the industrial revolution introduced new kinds of empires, new authorities propagated realities within a closed culture. Much like the ecosystem of a church that rules communities around it, industrial empires have created new authorities that support the aspiration of its hierarchy.

"A manufacturing plant could control the commerce of a town, while also controlling the tools and resources available to its inhabitants."

These community aberrations create a unified philosophy and *"way of life."* This *"way of life"* is translated into a unique version of social awareness. If it were beneficial to define day as *"night,"* or night as *"day,"* it would be so! Culture is established by acceptance of standards, usually defined by the church, enterprise, or ruling class.

It's about the regulation of ideas, where social reality can be very imposing. Based on the needs and desires of a controlling few, survival often relies on submission to the powerful. *"Survival of the Fittest"* can be better translated to *"Survival of the Adaptive."*

With each adaptation comes a circle of influence. With each influence comes acceptance of its own social reality.

"If you surrender to the will of the system, your reality becomes the system."

Our Physical Reality

There are many different influences that shape our daily reality! We spin our social awareness from norms and standards developed over time by our community.

However, the "physical world," also influences a unique perspective as well. Our dimensional reality spins the version of life that we see everyday. Something as simple as *"up and down"* can be very subjective. Depending on our vantage in time and space, will affect the perception of the world we see.

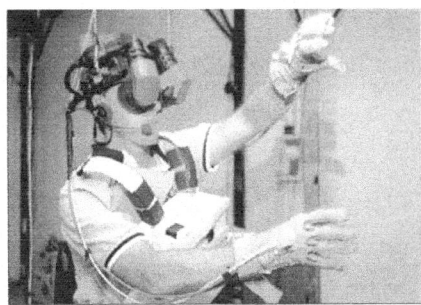

Astronauts on Skylab experienced total weightlessness, as suddenly direction has no meaning. Our bodily functions would morph and change as a result of this strange new environment. Gravity has been taken for granted, and has affected our motor impulses and biological makeup.

Another example of reality distortion is a story about three men moving a mirror. They drop it on the floor, and it breaks into a million pieces. The first man sees sun glistening off the edges of white and gold. The second man standing just two feet away, see green and blue dancing on the edge from a slightly different angle. Yet, a third man standing on Venus has not yet seen it break at all.

Time and vantage are most relevant in interpreting the state of any perception. Furthermore, perceptions can be clouded by a host of unforeseen variables, interpretations, and personal biases.

When did the mirror actually break..?

Undetermined. The first man cut himself. The second one did not. The third one from Venus doesn't know what you're talking about. The event has not yet happened from his perspective.

Did the mirror ever break...?

A case can be made that the mirror never broke at all. It all depends on perspective and your position when interpreting it.

If perception is personal, then reality must also be variable. Reality seems to be elastic like time and space itself. And if reality is variable, then what is the truth? Perhaps truth can also be variable. And if truth is variable, then perhaps God is variable too.

Each person has a unique and varied vantage in relationship with God. And that is simply how all religions can be right and wrong at the same time...

"Truth can be stated a thousand ways,
yet each one can be true."

—SWAMI VIVEKANANDA

Life of Illusion

As we pass through life, we often contemplate *what is real.*

The vision I hold for myself, is often skewed by alternative impressions from others. I can only perceive of what I am reflected against.

There are times, I wonder; if the mentally challenged ever know they are mentally challenged at all. At times, I wonder if I am simply humored by others without realization of my own mental limitations. Perhaps we are living life within a solitary straight jacket, only experiencing an existence, as we believe fully functional.

Moving through life and generating experiences may be nothing more than an invented awareness that suits our own perch. We live in biological straightjackets, and view our existence from a very limited set of tools. Those tools are forever changing as we advance with age and technology.

Our reflection is nothing more than a volatile backdrop.

"We live in a most flexible Universe."

WHAT ARE THE ANGLES?

Based on Einstein's concept of relativity, we know that the fabric of space and time is dynamic and flexible. It should be possible to beat a light ray to another sector of the galaxy by either wormhole or short-cut. Gravitational forces twisting the fabric of space-time could likely produce this phenomenon.

It's possible that one day we might engineer such warping via artificial gravity, or through natural gravitational forces like planets, moons, or black holes.

"In the future we might measure the degree of warping, and calculate relative time through actual distortions in space."

This would be a necessary adjustment in the same way we compensate for global time zones.

We will learn from the *"Circle People" in the next chapter*, that perception of awareness, and our place in this Universe, is extremely volatile. Depending on how we sense and make measurements, will determine what state, and **"when"** we can call **"now."**

In view of light driven perception, we know that light travels at an amazing 600 million miles per hour. Light can also move slower as its photons pass through natural cosmic filters, and dynamic gravities.

Photons move as both *waves* and as *particles*. As such, they emit an ongoing afterglow of *"cosmic radiation"* that forms a distinctive signature. *This could be described as a type of "aura" that could be witnessed from any vantage in the Universe.*

Depending on the number of reflections and the ultimate distance light travels, would affect any interpretation of an event. Because time and perception are variable, information delivered would be packaged in distinctive waves traveling forever like an echo. That is exactly what happens with radio signals and digital transmissions.

Theoretically, an observer on earth could measure any occurrence in the Universe, from any angle based on its light reflection. An event in your living room would be reflected against dozens of reflected objects, and skew the image being transferred. This alteration would affect time and the experience of the observer. The observer would build his or her own interpretation of what just happened.

Through a maze of reflections, one could observe any object as reflected light, and from any point in the Universe. Myself, sitting at my desk at home, would emit images of myself that could be captured through a complex series of reflections, perhaps detectable in Tokyo.

The sequence of events and its refracted light would become altered, thus painting a most distinctive picture. Each packet of light information would deliver a unique painting of myself, and be observable from any point in the Universe.

"Like an infinite camera in the sky."

Time portal from Star Trek,
"City on the edge of Forever"

Combining this so called *"camera"* with the warping of space- time itself, one could theoretically create a window in time by observing an event anywhere, and from any moment. In fact, anywhere we find light an observation could be made.

Imagine, advanced beings several light years from earth, observing our daily activities through a *"mirror-like-product,"* that collects photons from a very distant vantage point. Through the use of reflective conductors, they could look inside houses, under bridges, and observe the most minute corners of our world. *That would be quite a telescope!*

"The images captured, would be stretched, and distorted into something quite unique."

Boy with a Different Angle

I'd like to share a story about a young boy named Anthony, who lived on the edge of a mountain. He loved to paint and draw assorted images of hills just over the moors. As he watched each morning, the sun glistened across the hillside, casting shadows across the planes. At night, northern lights danced across the fog, stretching brilliant colors across the fall moonlight.

Each day he would pick up his canvas and paint what he saw. The problem was that, every day the picture looked very different. One morning he had purple mountains. The next day he would see enlarged peaks with sharp orange down slopes.

His teacher at the local art school had all 30 students draw the mountain from the window at the schoolhouse. And guess what.? All 30 kids drew a very different picture!

"The mountain is purple," "it is brown with white spots," "it is green with zebra stripes." A young blind boy said, *"it wasn't there at all."*

But Anthony always had the most unusual paintings of all. He owned an assortment of coke bottled glasses that could cast what ever image he wanted onto the landscape.

As a matter of fact, he owned a set of light deflecting sun lenses that added new arrays of rainbows to his stylish temples. *It was beautiful!*

He painted some of the most magnificent images that anyone has ever seen. The problem was, that no one knew what he was actually looking at.

They saw a cow. He saw a goat. They saw a mountain. He saw a Farris wheel. To make matters worse, Anthony painted what he saw last week, and from a tree house overlooking a reflecting pond. *Anthony was recognized as the local nut!*

One day Anthony sat gazing across the reflecting pond when a spaceship landed right under his tree. He chatted for a while, discussed the birds, and then received a mysterious little green box.

This little green box could capture light in *"slow-motion-time,"* and bounce signals from anywhere. He now could collect light beams and paint images from a mix of different time frames. *"A kind of kaleidoscope collector."*

This unit could slow light beams into fractional seconds, and extend moments on forever. With this device, Anthony could watch light travel from the bell tower to his home, back to his tree house, and on to the edge of the village.

Anthony bounced light from all kinds of directions, and every time he did, he would get a different balance of color. He noticed that if he bounced a reflection between mirrors, he could twist images and add warping curvatures. Based on the angle of attack, he could produce any image either right or left of the bell tower.

He asked a bystander on the street corner, to tell him where the potted plant next to the tower was. He asked; *"was it on the right or on the left?"* Every other time Anthony would trick him and move it back and forth. For a final observation, he exclaimed; *"Now tell me where*

the plant is right now." The bystander stood in horror. It was gone. Any light that was reflected from the plant was neutralized using stealth counter waves.

The bystander stood 30 feet away, and it was gone. He stood 10 feet and it was still gone. He reached out to touch it, and it suddenly appeared 10 feet to the left. At 30 and 10 feet, it didn't exist! At reaching distance, it appeared from another direction entirely.

What was the actual location of the plant?

Well, it kind of depends where you are observing it from.

Is the plant real?

It might be real somewhere, but not from where he was currently standing.

What color was the plant, and was it anywhere near the bell tower?

The color was always variable, and the bell tower happened to be 30 feet to the right at that time. The mountain in the background was nothing more than a hologram and never existed in the first place.

"So, it appears that light is probably a poor indicator of a stable reality."

Anthony further complicated matters by bouncing sound waves across the village at the same time. Sound waves echoed in all directions playing the same tricks as light. This leaves us with only the sense of touch for our confirmation.

Can we count on touch for our reality?

Touch is subject to the interaction of atomic force fields that repel molecules from touching each other. Matter expands and contracts based on heat energy delivered to electrons, and then organized into preferred orbital shells.

The make-up of matter is based on its atomic weight, its current energy level, and *"that exact moment"* in time and space. A train may have once steamed through your living room, but today you have a tree house. *"It's all a function of when."*

According to quantum mechanics, individual "particles" fly in and out of existence all the time. The fact is that we can never know the exact speed and location of a particle, implies that we should have serious doubts about our ability to determine reality based on the notion of touch and locality.

So, with all our basic senses in question, the only vantage of reality comes from our very limited human biology. Our brain absorbs perceptions and drafts an image of all human reality. This appears to be only a small slice of the range of potential encounters, but also, the only reality that is relevant to us.

We live within our minds, and we generate life from within a very limited crawlspace. And I guess the real question is not if it is real, but; **is it actually real to you?**

Anthony continued to bounce light from all directions. He created images and distortions that generated images of all kinds… *"Elephants," "Tanks," "Space Ships,"* and all his efforts shocked and amazed his audience.

One man in the crowd yelled; *"Hey that's not real!"* Anthony responded; what do you mean it's not real. Is a photon any less real than a particle? Particles are made of quarks that move in and out of existence all the time.

Are photons less real than quarks? Is matter and light, the same thing?

The same force **"electromagnetism"** energizes both holograms and matter. That force is delivered by photons, and generates light energy when collided with electrons.

The energized electrons redirect and transmit carrier light waves, while at the same time, causing electrons to jump to the next higher orbit. It's from those negatively charged orbits of electrons, that repel atoms from touching each other. This is what gives us the illusion of matter.

So, you can't actually touch anything. Just its force field!

Images that you see are subject to angle of attack and the distortion of light refraction. All matter is simply the repulsion of electrons. Otherwise, matter is mostly empty space.

Our own essence actually moves in and out of phase, as we navigate through this electromagnetic force of nature. The solidity of our bodies, are that of heat energy as we interact with the forces in our environment.

"It all adds up to a most surreal Universe."

The Transmission of Touch

There are **five** human senses that connect our world with reality. We have established a multitude of instruments that can stretch information beyond our capabilities, but these are outside of our direct observation.

In establishing reality, we utilize only what connects directly with our brain's capability. Unfortunately, taste and smell add very little human receptive value. Therefore, our window to the Universe is predominately based on sight, sound, and touch.

Everything in our Universe is ruled by force fields that regulate the interaction of molecules that make up matter.

The reason we don't fall through the earth from the tug of gravity, is the fact that our sub-atomic particles, emit a repellent force, that buffers entry into adjacent space.

The strong force holds the nucleus together, while its orbiting electrons protect the integrity of its air space. Light energy is transmitted by photons carried on that same electro-magnetic wave.

As photons strike electrons, heat energy is produced, that further increase its repulsive sub-atomic barrier. Each element is courted with specific atomic weight. Electrons dance forever until invited to bond with the next adjacent particle.

Our sense of touch is simply those repellent forces pushing particles in and out of the way. Our sense of vision is skewed by our position. Time then affects the movement of these repellant forces, and all light fabrication. Reality becomes an ongoing construct of observation.

In summary, photons bomb our world from all directions and from all angles. Light from its electro-mechanical spectrum projects appearance of everything that is real. The electron's repulsion is what gives all matter its physical definition.

What we do know is that both sight and touch are regulated by interaction of photons with electrons. The more we learn about this interaction, the less certain we should be about anything we can see and touch.

"All things are subject to interpretation. Whichever interpretation prevails is a function of perception and not truth." — *Friedrich Nietzsche*

When quantum physicists stumbled upon the **Double Slit Experiment,** they were in for a shock. This famous quantum experiment shows how tiny particles behave differently when they are actually being measured!

It seems that until we observe reality, it only exists as a range of probabilities. The act of making a measurement collapses this range, and makes reality "choose" a defined path of action.

The Double Slit Experiment uses an electron gun to fire individual particles onto a screen. When *"observed,"* the results show a *"particle pattern,"* as expected from matter. Physical matter should leave a physical trace.

However, when the firing was *"unobserved,"* the backdrop on the screen resulted in a *"wave pattern."* This experiment demonstrated thousands of times, suggests that conscious observation affects the outcome. In order to produce these results, the observation would had to have happened prior to the electron gun firing. This is an example of when the *"present"* influences the past, and delivers a different result.

If observations can be bent, then its measurement can be subject to alterations in its delivery. And that alteration in delivery can drive its effect, prior to its original cause. Such a paradox generates a timeless loop by confusing the order of action and consequence.

Is matter a wave or a particle?

SYNCHRONICITY

And Elastic Universe

Cause and effect, and the order that we receive information, is most relevant in defining our Universe.

As a butterfly lands on a flower, its petals fall off and land in the mud. The rain moves the peddles into a marsh, where it breaks down and nourishes the soil with carbon microbes.

A worm is the beneficiary of the nourishment and multiplies into a food supply for a nearby family of frogs. Frogs lay eggs, and the cycle has an ongoing effect on that habitat.

Now if the butterfly was slightly delayed, or its time and motion were somehow altered, it might miss the petal all together, the petal never falls, and nourishment is never provided.

If the butterfly and the petal meet at just the right junction of time and space, a cell is fertilized. The family chain has a chance to develop, and thus consciousness lives on. If the fertilization is missed, or a timely sparrow eats the egg, nothing becomes alive.

Consciousness never awakens and survives.

I have always joked about a force somehow mocking me.

It seems that every time I am late or in a hurry, something unexpected seems to happen! I lose my keys, forgot to put gas in the car… The dog decides to take her own sweet time to do business in the yard… Whatever can happen will! And the slogan *"shit happens"* seems to ring true.

As I drive to work, there are always cars in my path. I don't know why, but sometimes it appears that the world is a stage, with actors leaping into my path, and deviating my life. I get on the highway, and a farm truck decides at just that moment, to swing into my lane. *"A full 15 miles per hour!"*

At just that moment in the intersection that usually has no traffic at all, there is a parade of cars… red… now white… two more gray… and oh yes, the light turns red again.

I have driven this path a hundred times before, and there has never been any traffic here. But, when I'm in a hurry, the parade decides to begin.

I stop into McDonald's to get a cup of coffee. There is a huge line. As I finally get to the front, there is absolutely no one behind me. Of course, I get the cashier who doesn't know how to count change, and forgets to pick up my order at the window! An elderly man decides to start talking to me, and in politeness, I lose another 5 minutes.

So, the Universe of action or inaction is compliant only if the host and inducer cross the same path. And while everything moves at different rates and tempos through the Universe, an affect is brought about by the intersection of two coordinates in time and space.

However, the action of *synchronicity* may only be viable in a mechanical world of which we observe.

We know that matter crosses in and out of position all the time. Matter that moves in and out of different planes or *"Universes,"* affects what takes place in ours… *Much like the effects, we feel from gravity!*

It is believed that gravity is disbursed throughout multiple dimensions. And so, if our Universe is influencing others.., then perhaps we also are influencing "alternative Universes."

We are regularly receiving dialogue so to speak, with other dimensions.

If our ancestors live on in a different plane of existence, they may inadvertently affect us in the here and now. Actions in time and space carry on, and live in multiple dimensionalities.

"Forward" and *"backwards"* as the peddle rises up, and the butterfly launches up and away. Some actions run opposite each other. So, the petal might fall up, and the butterfly flies down and collides a fraction earlier. An alternative event has been created.

According to Isaac Newton, there is an equal and opposite reaction to all events. That may only be true in a Newtonian world of which we think we live.

Einstein later proved that Newton's interpretation might not be correct. The world is not synchronized like a large clock, but rather has warps, bends, and distortions. As particles interact, they prove a range of possible actions. Not everything moves in the same direction all at once.

The flow of time moves like a river in current. Some currents move faster, and sometimes in opposing directions. This unique flexibility creates a Universe of distortions, and thus will interchange *"cause and effect."*

The long-standing theory, *"every action has an equal and opposite reaction,"* supports a traditional view of an exact synchronized world.

We are now discovering that there are far too many moving parts, and too many potential outcomes. While one relation-ship may affect another, the predicted outcomes are more like an assortment of possibilities.

Synchronicity can never be assured or predicted. While we rely on synchronicity in our linear existence, the grander scope of the Universe does not necessarily follow that order at all. *It often thrives on disorder.*

Those who seek synchronicity in life, often seek order in astrology or religion as well. *But remember,* the stars won't tell us the proper crop cycle, or when a baby is to be born. It may impact billions of events, but these effects are quite random and in multiple directions.

In addressing a fundamental question;

Do you acknowledge synchronicity?

The answer must be; *"I believe in cause and effect, and I also believe in effect on effect! And we can never be sure of which order we receive them."*

Intersection of fate

Each action fans out into new paths of multiple realities.

Altering an event produces alternative courses, each with its own assortment of possibilities. Similar to the branching of a tree, each generation creates its own intersection of time and space. Such intersections weave their own progression through history, until it meets the next encounter.

The warping effect of time from each element of travel can produce a multitude of collisions and a multitude of alternative outcomes. Those alternative outcomes may best describe the vast range of multifaceted encounters.

So, the question becomes, do you prefer a bearded Spock or a shaven one? *"A living cat or a dead one in a box?"*

"A living spirit or a finite human existence?"

All good questions with no absolute answer!

"Spock in alternative reality"
Star Trek, Mirror, Mirror

Quantum Possibilities

In recent decades, quantum physics has opened the door to new and subtle possibilities. Quantum mechanics has launched new ideas of *"supernatural forces," "life after death experiences,"* and the ability to make "reality" conform to an unlimited range of possibilities.

Questions for consideration might include:

1. Do the principles of quantum physics also apply to the everyday "macro" level of human reality?

2. Is quantum entanglement the key to telepathy, instantaneous communication, or instant teleportation to anywhere in the cosmos?

3. Does quantum physics conflict with the concept of synchronicity, or do they complement each other?

4. Does quantum physics support the notion that the mind creates all of reality?

5. Does quantum physics support the existence of ghosts and other non-corporeal entities?

6. Are we living in a "Holographic Universe" projected from only a two dimensional reality?

7. Can we be both alive and dead at the same time?

How Do We Know Were Alive?

In writing this book, we have looked at several fundamental issues related to our living awareness. Reality may be nothing more than an individualized painting derived from a limited set of biological senses.

We know that **touch** or *"feeling"* in human beings, can be modified with the use of simple drugs. In some cases, nerve endings can be deadened creating a numb *"non-feeling"* experience. Interaction with outside physical matter would be limited at best!

Repellent forces at the atomic level float your molecules like a boat drifting in water. This further complicates an exact point of reference, or even an exact point in time. The physical Universe is endlessly distorted, and defies hard definition.

Electro-magnetic light energy can be bent and distorted from the reflective angles produced. Our current snapshot of refracted light is not only individualistic, but paints a slightly different picture for each person observing it.

"The world is but a canvass to our imagination."

—HENRY DAVID THOREAU

Light is received from many different angles, and its collective, paints a unique perception of the here and now.

Our reception of **sound** or *"sound vibrations,"* is only relevant through air or some similar earthly conductor. Sound has no meaning outside our human envelope, and is only processed through our brain's interpretation. Taste and smell have these similar limitations, and are subject to the same human chemistry.

So, what connects our vital window to reality?

I have always maintained that our physical reality is not as reliable as we think. Our awareness stems not from physical sensory, but rather from our ideas and concepts that fill our spiritual identity.

"Our identity may be variable like the Universe itself.
One's perception of them self, is seldom what others
perceive about them."

— M Z

I can only evaluate what is in my own head, and that evaluation comes from experiences nurtured through my own interpretation. While I have extracted concepts of the world from which I live, I am not sure those experiences, are strictly influenced by the limitations of only my five senses.

Because human beings have become so volatile in their perceptions of the world around them, they have bridged the difference with religious faith and spiritual interpretations.

"And that's not necessarily a bad thing!"

Humans appear to be more than the sum of their physical existence. They have utilized innate skills and programming both through their DNA, and their ongoing spiritual lineage. And that connection may best describe the conduit to the world around us!

THE CIRCLE PEOPLE

An Alternative Universe

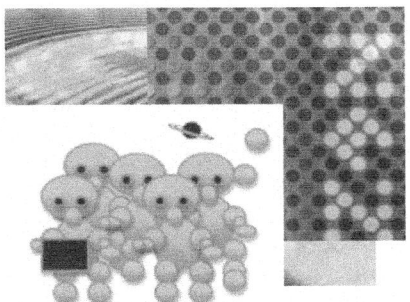

I'd like to share a story about a young man who traveled to a strange and distant land. A place where human speech was not tolerated, and daylight was most frowned upon.

This young man, let's call him "IP-782," was commanded by town elders to learn the local language, and submit to the current labor force. All residents were relegated to stripping colors from light images, and drawing little black circles to cover all remaining light.

His teacher and interpreter began the indoctrination process. She first educated him on the language of black circles. Then she guided him to a little black box, where he was instructed to place his head. *"Old ways must be re-learned,"* she said. *"You are never allowed to remove your head from this box, or you will face certain annihilation."*

You are required from now on, to only use the language of our land, and to generate little black circles in a box. You will be nourished through an electrical connection attached to your side, and we will inject a substance that numbs your nervous system and sensory.

From now on, you will live in a black box and make black circles in order to communicate. As your body degenerates, you will remain only in our world of dark circles. As the eons pass, you will become a member of our Universe where you will live out all your living experiences.

Duration and distance will have no meaning. You will soon lose all concepts of light, structure, and dimensionality, as you once knew it. You will now live among the circle people.

You will only hypothesize the concept of light, and never interact with this elusive dimension. Light will become only theory, as you will no longer have any interaction with this phenomenon. In our dark gray world, we live only in black holes, and curved dimensions.

The next day IP-782, woke from his dream and reclaimed his name as William. He basked in the sunshine and smelled the roses on his windowsill.

As he gathered his resume that morning, and ventured out to the nearest state job office, he was instructed that they could no longer accept paper applications.

The only way to communicate with the State, and its exclusive job market, is to submit through a little black box, and become a citizen of the new virtual state.

William was advised, that they would never again accept phone inquiries or in-face personal visits. The State office will only recognize those who speak directly through this little black box, and appropriately identify themselves. His new identity shall be IP-782.

On the way home, he noticed several retail stores, a school, and an old entertainment village, boarded up. There was no street activity at all.

If IP-782 needed anything at all, he would have to order it on- line. All interactions, education, and entertainment, must now be furnished through his personal black box, designed and manufactured of course, by the Black Circle Corporation.

And because he had been out of work and unable to pay the connection charge, he ran the risk of being terminated.

Explained by his job councilor, *"you must speak only through the little black box. You must learn correct code and always identify yourself as IP-782. From now on, you will not be recognized in any other manor."*

As the years passed, more and more reliance became essential with this box. The next generation pledged total allegiance as they were plugged in right from the cradle.

As their human senses began to fail, those who were most adept with the black box survived and prospered. Eyesight and hearing became totally unnecessary. The sense of touch was only a thing of the past. The reality for IP-782's children, who were assigned IP-766, and IP-767, morphed into a daily relationship with this unit. "Reality" for them was inside this device, not out-there.

After a few more generations had passed, a new fundamental Universe was created *"A New Genesis."* As the Universe of old became less and less *"real,"* the language of code became the salvation for relationships and all vision of reality.

Mobility is no longer important. Light a minor inconvenience. The sense of touch is irrelevant. The surviving species of our time are those who best absorb code, and have a personality best suited for this little black box!

Are we the circle people?

Corporations invented and birthed the black box within our living Universe. This Universe is real, and absolutely essential for survival within our society. Today computers serve as a comprehensive source for all our interpersonal relationships, education, information, and monitoring.

This brave new world holds the potential of trapping its inhabitants as a necessary evil for survival. The character of our Universe is forever changing. We are forever evolving.

Over time, our sensory will be re-prioritized as we develop new tools that experience the world around us. Our most critical variable for survival may be our integration with this box. Our daily awareness will be that of electronic stimuli, as our only exclusive contact with the Universe.

Are we falling down a rabbit hole?

We view our world from three dimensions of space, and one of time. We hypothesize as many as seven more dimensions may be curled up in space according to superstring theory.

Dark matter may pose yet more dimensional possibilities, as light waves splinter into countless bridges of super space, whether we perceive it or not. The mere fact that we have evidence of black holes, presents a true reality of altered places and times.

Complex frequencies, particularly in the electrical-mechanical realm, assure millions of possibilities. Our newest Universe created and monitored by man, may well be the little black box we experience as cyberspace.

"The rabbit hole is as deep as we have dug it."—Gary Hopkins

How We Interpret Reality

We as humans are locked into experiences from only five senses. For without these senses, we would have no way of perceiving the world around us or developing any kind of understanding of reality.

If just one sense were absent or weakened, the remaining senses would project a different symphony of reality. A blind person may be more dominantly focused on sound, or the sensation of touch, rather than sight. All senses are experienced most uniquely.

The range of human perception is very limited. Humans see only about 2% of actual light waves generated. The fact is, that we really don't know how wide the spectrum expands in both directions. From ultra red, to blue gamma rays.

Consequently, we don't know how slow a wave can travel over space, or how fast a frequency can be accelerated.

Sound faces many of the same unknowns, as there are also unique timber vibrations that give sound its character.

"Sound waves never die, they persist, fainter and fainter, masked by the day-to-day noise of the world."

—GUGLIELMO MARCONI

We have not yet defined dark matter, or dark energy, although we know it dominates our space. We know it exists, but we have no way of detecting it. Dark matter will likely reveal new windows into our perception and dimensional awareness.

Animals within our own familiar family of senses have varied abilities that stretch the vast mix of perception. What is heard by my cocker spaniel as reality of fact, my human ears never heard it! *In my universe, the sound never happened.*

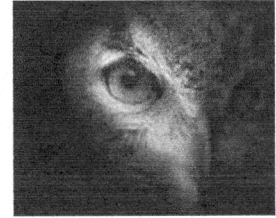

The art of being wise, is knowing where to look. —William Janson

Perception can be further enhanced through advanced *"tools"* or *"instruments,"* that further extend our natural abilities. We can see only as far as our tools and perceptions will take us. *Today, we are most dependent on these tools!*

Broader perception can be advanced through such things like electric mechanical impulses, DNA coding, gravity detection, time dilation, thermal reactions, etc... All these measurements would illuminate new dimensional possibilities, and affect the way we see the Universe.

The range of perception is unlimited. Each sensory spins its own version of reality. Each observation generates its own tapestry Universe, and interpretation.

As a species, we are moving into a cybernetic Universe with each passing day. A world where individual expression doesn't matter. Only cold hard data, text messaging, emails, or code will suffice.

We are creating a culture of non-verbal communication, and isolating our existence behind screens of electronic firewalls. Human interaction is changing. And as we continue to do so, we are moving into a world of individual isolation and collective conditioning.

My fear is that emotion, arts, and science will become de-valued in the process. *"Individuality"* or *"political will,"* may become a thing of the past. Survival of the fittest relies increasingly on *"uniformity"* and *"information extraction,"* by those specified electronic boxes. These boxes are the plugs to our working reality, our art, and our new living awareness.

Today, people no longer make phone calls. Fewer seek personal inter-action, and fewer socialize. When someone reaches out in a traditional manor, the recipient is often on guard of ulterior motive.

Traditional sales in the workplace is unwarranted, and seen as an offensive gesture. A phone call today is questioned as to *"Why are you calling me?"*

The new renaissance man of the future will be pluggable and adapt-able. Supportive of the hive mentality, from our social media society, he must be willing to accept the next program designated through corporate sponsors.

Communications will be limited to code. Reality will be limited to accesses to this little black box. Our pigeonhole to the Universe will be the conduit that gives us our sliver of light.

AN ILLUSION FOR CONTROL

"Our Social Reality"

"Governments should serve people, not institutions."
We should not be shy about demanding policies that benefit
the majority. Only a corrupt government prioritizes the desires
of the few over the needs of its people."

—THOMAS JEFFERSON

**"Capitalism will invariably lead to
economic consolidation."**
That consolidation will ultimately lead to a lack of competition
and innovation in the marketplace, where products and
services would otherwise compete."

—BART BICKLEMAN

"The top 1% of Americans own 52% of the nation's wealth."
The top 400 equal the lowest 65% of the nation..."

—JOSEPH STIGLITZ ECONOMIST

Illusion for Control

From the time we are born, we are conditioned to crave a designed acceptance of *"commercialism," (buy this, sell that)*, and learn a philosophical brand of what's *"right and wrong."*

In our society, it's correct to be capitalistic, to support the acquisition of property, and to become the ultimate consumer!

We are led into working agendas, that further support the goals directed by the ruling empires of our society.

Our security is based not on wellness, stimulation, or Karma, but rather procedure, financial accumulation, and uniformity. Legally, materially, and most persuasively, those who hold power will prescribe the direction and reality of our lifetime activities.

Without recognition, we conform to this system, craving what is presented, while etching a world view around what has been furnished.

The root of our political, social and value systems are simply a fabrication for control. Not unlike that of religious formula.

"It's about regulation of ideas and thoughts in our society, that ultimately discourage outside thinking."

Whenever new ideas do surface, it is usually because its supportive of the established monetary system. ***Innovation and science are regimented by strict rules!*** Unwittingly we accept its influence, and join into the established cause.

Private business clubs emerge across our landscape. Often keeping the general public out, they conduct their private mission, while preying on the society around them. They hide behind corporate veils of privacy, as they invent their own rules for membership.

Acceptance takes shape in blurred concepts of values.

- *Corporate welfare over individual welfare.*

- *Mergers so big, they control the products and resources available to you.*

- *The sacrifice of privacy in the wake of commercial enterprise's right to know.*

- *Marketers directing appeal into generic bundles for public consumption.*

- *When the only recreation available, is often sponsored and profited by someone else.*

These adaptations should begin to concern us! *"Are we becoming inoculated by society?"*

Perhaps real education is better reached through self-exploration, as opposed to traditional established disciplines. We should be more focused on *"Karma,"* or a path that brings us greater self-realization. Are we unwittingly enslaving our souls?

The following exemplifies the condition:

A handicapped woman being told by her employer; *"Can you smile a little bigger please? If you can't force happiness, we need to let you go! It's bad for our image as one big happy family."*

A quadriplegic with no arms or legs, begging for change outside Caesar's Palace's gambling facility and told to "move along."

The simple statement *"No trespassing allowed!"*

"Corporate persuasion in government is acceptable, but foreign influence will not be tolerated."

Sports casual day at work means everyone can dress alike. It's been mandated to dress down. "What a benefit."

We have become soldiers in life. For some reason beyond my understanding, we spend a considerable amount of time and energy, controlling each other. Our acceptance of the formula has delivered this current condition.

"Conformity cannot be the journey of an expanding soul." —MZ

Our Version of America

In 1776, prestigious leaders of the colonies baited revolution. Their efforts were a means of ensuring **ownership** in the name of free enterprise, **tax relief** for asset owners, and a **banking system** to be run by those instigating revolution in the first place. Wealthy colonists, often with the most to gain, promoted aggressive change on the backs of rank and file colonists.

The American Revolution was simply a grand family feud.

It was clear that monarchies of Europe were all closely related, and often at war with each other. The American Revolution simply perpetuated this wonderful tradition, at the expense of Blacks, Indians, or anyone else that got in their way.

From the beginning of colonial America, the founders, leaders, and high sheriffs, were representatives of the King. These privileged families just happened to gain the most land, wealth, and power in the colonies. It was this same group, that later became the leaders and legislators that led to our American Revolution. Often with the most at stake, they influenced political movement through owned newspapers, and political advantage.

Those very bloodlines launched our first presidents. Often intermarried *-a bit like royalty*, they legislated from a position of rank and power.

Years later Robert E. Lee, *"also related to Washington and Custis,"* propagated the southern rebellion. He was uniquely positioned to be the great leader and confederate General that we all read about. It was an amazing coincidence, that this "General" with all the privilege of education, wealth, and rank, was also connected to the first Revolutionary families, as well as the British Monarchy.

Today, our governmental leaders seem to have related bloodlines, and often have a better than average chance to continue their leadership.

Should an average person be thrust into this same position of authority, such as the men we read about in history books, we would be reading about very different heroes…

A country for and by the people is *"power-speak,"* from a government seeking to protect the interest of an established few. We should recognize who is leading us, and stop worshiping those who ration our limited resources back to us. **"We conceptualize only what we have accepted!"**

Nothing is more relevant than the divisions we see today in our politics. For some reason, we have morphed our attitude and ideals, consistent with those delivering the message.

Our once free press has become dominated by all kinds of special interests and profitable intent. We have homogenized our news in shaded buckets of truth. We have seen mergers and acquisitions of the most powerful, and they have shaped the brands and information delegated to us.

Today, political attitudes have consolidated around only two major parties, with distinct platforms and a distinct audience. Therefore, we are seeing construction of a polarized truth.

This force is very hard to combat. I find myself mesmerized with repetition, and the stacking of attitudes with a specific point of view. There is nothing new here, however, this reality can pose great dangers for our ultimate well-being and search for truth. We all live within our domed realities.

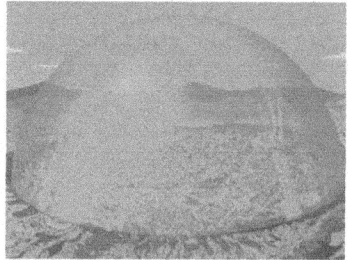

VASTNESS OF LANDSCAPE

As we explore the undeniable influences that social norms bring our society, we should also recognize how the physical world also dominates our reality.

We have been conditioned to think of our world in traditional formulas. "We are the center of the Universe." "God revolves around the Earth." In our world we have "up & down," "right & wrong," "this way or that," "past or present," and even "living or dead!"

Our science measures a light year in terms of an *"earthly"* year around the sun. This standard is compared against a variable time backdrop, *and* of only our visible Universe.

(A light year is measured from where?)

The point is that we have created and shaped a version of our own reality that fits our perspective. Everything we do, from our value systems to our concept of the world, is not only restrictive, but is the result of slanted conditioning over many thousands of years. **We can think no other way!**

"Dimensional awareness is a mindset."

—MZ

As we begin to absorb the grand enormity and scale of our physical world, we continue to understate the vastness of this rich expansive Universe.

Like bandwidths on a radio with millions of frequencies, our spatial reality is further complicated by billions of warped planes and vantages that intersect all points in space/time. *(General Relativity)*

Infinite planes move through the cosmos at different rates and times. They bend to their own frequency, held together in a grid of attracted matter. That's similar to how radio signals work.

Each *"prism of light,"* casts its own shade of reality. Likewise, we also cast our own course through the cosmos. The realm of our Universe is flexible beyond our wildest dreams. What is understood as, billions of light years are also, billions of multi-dimensional adjustments. The possibilities are unlimited!

By acknowledging such grander, our deeper understanding of the metaphysical world in which we live becomes infinitely more complicated. The traditional view of God and heavens becomes vastly more restrictive. Our appreciation for religious transcript can be less satisfying.

In reference to theology, what gives us the right to say; "The lord is one," "God speaks through our prayers," "Jesus died for our sins," or that the "Torah has *any relevance to God what-so-ever.*"

Our 10 commandments the bedrock of our belief system, neglect many critical rules for society. While supportive of civilization, it does not encourage any positive pro-active commitments such as; *"Love others.., seek happiness.., encourage others.., seek knowledge.., consume yourself in imagination.., or make a difference in your lifetime."*...

A list from God as it stands, would seem very incomplete. *Instead, it refers to wrath, to honor & obey, and accept no others...*

We can define only a few certainties from our limited perspective:

1. The will to survive and seek knowledge is programmed into our being. *It has been handed down as absolute law.*

2. Take advantage of each phase of reality because anything beyond is never guaranteed. (If you find pleasure, take it! If you find discomfort, change it!)

3. Greater understanding is always around the corner. Pursue it, and never be satisfied with the current understanding of truth.

4. Challenge the system. Grow create and evaluate. *(It's by these means that one can break the blindness of the current condition, and seek beyond.)*

5. *There is order to the Universe!*

Intelligent Design

(Ultimate Responsibility)

For the sake of conversation, lets accept intelligent design as our established belief, and that God *(a supreme being),* is directing our journey. Under this premise, God is ultimately accountable for good and evil, justice and injustice, guidance and leadership throughout the Universe.

We should be grateful for the gift of life, stimulation, and awareness, however when circumstances take on negative consequences, we could feel justified in issuing blame.

We might not understand all the motives behind an event, however, from a traditional worship perspective, we would be expected to make sacred judgments on *"right and wrong," "suffering and healing."*

We hold God to an ultimate standard, and expect him to deliver that high expectation. However, in many instances our traditional God delivers a threshold far below what has been assigned. If we are compelled to follow his ideals, we should expect nothing less in return. For without such lofty standards, the Universe and his kingdom would be a less significant place.

"When expectations are not met in accordance with given value systems, we should have a right to hold the creator accountable."

From a traditional worship perspective, God holds undeniable responsibility, as do we. *"After all, we are interdependently linked!"* As stated earlier we are a part of the "multiplex," and a component of God. The responsibility should work in both directions!

Theist and Deist

The **Theist** believes in the existence of one or more Gods, which dominate the Universe. God interacts with the Universe and is invincible and all encompassing. God is the creator of the human race, and overshadows everything in the world.

A **Deist** believes that God created the Universe, but does not necessarily intervene in it. **God** remains separate and apart, while exercising its power through natural laws. God reveals itself through nature and reason, not revelation. The Bible is not considered the infallible word of God.

Since the 18th century, Deism has used science to justify its stance. Scientists, like Isaac Newton, were better able to explain how the Universe actually worked. Many mysteries formerly attributed to God, yielded simple and mechanistic explanations. Some Deists also ventured into atheism, which is a belief of no God at all. Science has regularly engaged in this ongoing battle with religion for the hearts and minds of man.

The Atheist

(Lack of Evidence)

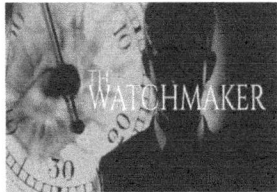  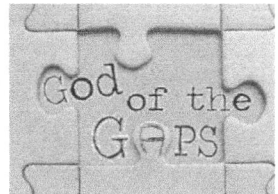

There are many misunderstood concepts and labels given to people of both faith and non-faith. The concept of atheism is perhaps one of the most misunderstood of all.

From an atheistic perspective, *"God cannot exist without verifiable and creditable evidence."* It is that lack of evidence that diminishes the value and opportunity for the language of God.

God can take many forms and definitions, from many different people. While it might be easy to discount the God of the Bible, it may not be so easy to dismiss the existence of a spiritual bond with the Universe, or a higher authority for its laws in motion.

My defense of God is because I believe inspiration is real, and humans have demonstrated amazing abilities beyond logical limitations. While we might dismiss fables of the handwritten bible, we cannot dismiss the value of inspiration or motivation that seem to rule our human experience.

We are spiritual creatures, and have a long history of multiple civilizations, in adapting beliefs as a mechanism of survival. **Perhaps belief is an adaptive necessity.**

The intangibles of life, described by Aristotle as *"Ether,"* demonstrated as far back as the 4th century B.C., an acute awareness of forces beyond our physical environment.

The mere fact that the laws of nature are set in motion and never change, demonstrate a finite order, and structure to our living Universe. Together, with human inspiration, we unveil a unique bond between man and the cosmos.

The fact that there is historical precedence in all civilizations, and at all times with religion, demonstrates an ongoing and continuous relationship as a human experience.

God can exist when viewed in context of infinite possibilities, and continues to demonstrate itself in a unique relationship with man. That relationship, logically, can be anything that it is established to be, as God has no limitations.

Science is now scratching the edge of our Universe. We are gaining new insight into the quantum world and so many other new disciplines. We are discovering new definitions of time, relativity, and dimensionality. And we are humbling ourselves in the process as we discover the vastness of our great unknowns. The flexible concept of God certainly seems to be a case in reality.

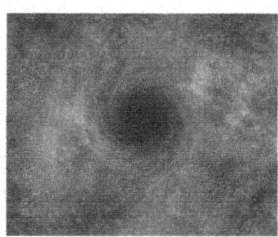

OUR PHYSICAL UNIVERSE

In All the Cosmos

How vast is the cosmos? Astronomers estimate our galaxy is 100,000 light years across, with our closest Star, Alpha Centauri four light years away. We know there are probably 100 billion galaxies just like ours, with more discovered every day.

Light travels an amazing 186,000 miles per second, a most astronomical distance in one year. (186,000 X 60 seconds X 60 Minutes X 24 Hours X 365 days) = **1 light year.**

At such speed, the laws of matter may alter, punching holes into new dimensional realities. Anti-matter, *gravitational crush of black holes,* punch into yet more regions of the cosmos.

Only 10 percent of visible matter exists in our Universe.

90 percent is dark matter and falls outside the realm of our visible reality.

Size and time relationships of traveling matter opens yet further possibilities. *"The Atoms could be planets, the galaxies complex molecular structures for something else."*

With such grander and awesome magnificence, Gods rule is truly beyond our earthly claims.

Travels of the Water

As a stream of water flows downward to a puddle, the frog in the puddle concludes that it's the Java's great command that water flows down nourishing his family of frogs.

But then suddenly the puddle fills upward changing the laws of the flow.

Now he concludes water can move up or down and can over run the pond into the vast creek bed beyond. *And it was good!* And the streams led to oceans with new creatures and new motions. The oceans fill packing darkness underneath, as the surface evaporates towards the sun releasing its vapor air born. *The rules continue to change!*

And as water molecules merge and collide, they create other structures to ride away with comets and magnetic pulls in the sky. As the journey of change precedes through the cosmos, like a pin ball dancing against the light, *the envelope of rules keep changing.*

"Command" has been altered. "*Purpose*" has been expanded. The frog's awareness "irrelevant."

What seemed right by the stream, has no significance to the travels of the water ....

Lyrics from the song "Travels of the Water" —MZ

Touching Alien Worlds

As we view our world from a variety of social and physical perspectives, we continue to witness just how limited our vantage really is.

Our experience builds on physiological and mental interpretations of the world around us. We also develop an identity in the inspirational world as well. We have formed tendencies that have passed through the generations, and have reinforced a familiar mindset.

There is an argument to be made that rituals and habits over time find their way into the DNA developmental genome. Human traits such as happiness, unconscious mannerisms, eating habits, rituals, all have a direct influence on future generations.

The question becomes; if a vast isolated civilization, had formed eons of their own habits, lifestyle, belief systems, and environment influences.., would we recognize any aspect of their social behavior at all?

We humans have established a world vision from a familiar perspective! We have established ideals and standards for *"life as we know it,"* but have never stretched beyond earthly man-made interpretations.

In consideration of all the living possibilities, we share very similar experiences in this very isolated corner of the cosmos. Despite a similar environment, we still see such diversity as *"Insects and elephants," "oak trees and birds," "fish and grass," "amino acids and bacteria."* All these examples seem most un-relatable.

Imagine the infinite possibilities of wider cosmic diversity, vaster time frames, or countless new dimensions. We might further stretch natural laws, as we have recognized them.

Extraterrestrial entities outside our world would face very different and unique challenges. Many conditions would be most unfamiliar. Variables might include; variations in gravity, atmospheric pressures, or extreme temperatures. We likely would see unique biological and chemical adaptations, imposed by vast eco-systems, or by a range of complex environments.

Other influences might include ultraviolet/radiant exposures, planetary rotations, centrifugal forces, vast differences in spatial sizes, or micro-forces that surround space-time itself.

Relative speed-of-motion through the Universe pose yet more variables affecting our awareness. *"Civilizations might be riding through us so fast as to escape detection."*

We should also consider the possibility that "consciousness," may exist among inanimate objects, and physical matter itself. There appears to be new evidence related to this.

With so much diversity to consider, the results would likely produce a variety of entities, vastly different from anything we could imagine.

"Alien inhabitants" would likely be:

a. **Different** in appearance, from anything we would be familiar with.

b. **Unrecognizable,** to anything we might look for.

c. **Incommunicable,** as here on earth most species cannot communicate between themselves.

d. **Unpredictable,** from human and animal emotional responses as we have learned them.

Humanoid aliens as depicted in movies would seem most unlikely. Time disparity, inter-dimensionality, speed-motion by-pass, or vast differences in evolution, would make recognition almost impossible.

Emotional tendencies have been ingrained into our cellular fabric, and thus we are born with pattern instincts passed down from our origins. Such chemistry has bound our being into predictably reactive creatures. **Without the benefit of centuries of evolution, our expressive make-up would be vastly different.**

Chariots of the Gods

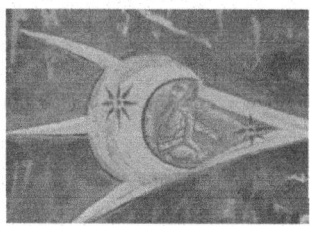 

It's fun to fantasize about aliens once helping our civilization. However, I'm not sure we needed that helping hand. At the rate of observable advances in technology, it's conceivable that humans have made their own breakthroughs. Sometimes, even regressing the science, and stepping back in technology.

Deducing from the uniqueness of alien possibilities, extra-terrestrial encounters would likely be far different from anything we would recognize on earth. *"Beings"* who arise from a wide range of evolutionary origins, would resemble nothing close to our own definition of life.

The idea that **ancient aliens** once seeded our population, or that we are biologically related, is a stretch of evolutionary understanding. From the vast range of eco-systems, *"not always similar to ours,"* I question the viability of non-related *"entities,"* adapting from so many different environments.

Seeding our world makes little sense. Aliens would have to engineer just the right offspring, with just the right eco-system. Based on evidence of evolution, and the vast trials that start and end, it is unlikely that *"just the right seeds,"* would be implemented to produce the outcomes we see today.

Alien existence would hold little resemblance to our own biological family. Results would likely demonstrate a range of unthinkable creatures with very little relatable similarity.

"Alien life is quite common in the Universe, although intelligent life is less so. Some say it has yet to appear on planet Earth."

—STEPHEN HAWKING

So, we observe the human creature that we know today.

A creature of habit and machine-like tendencies. We see a host of involuntary responses, and a likeness of creative thinking that bleeds across the millennium.

A kind of programming that bridges our future, and baits a quest for more understanding.

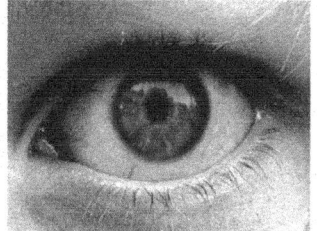

OUR HUMAN MACHINE

After observing several subtle traits from related families,

I have noticed some very interesting tendencies. Certain nervous habits seem to run within families, such as pawing one's hair, or a mild twitch in the corner of the eye.

I can't imagine what kind of mechanism would cause me to twitch in a most specific way, or my dog to wag his tail when happy. *"I certainly have no natural impulse to shake my lower spine."*

It appears that the brain is wired very specifically through the genetic process. Wiring is created from birth, and directs the flow of consciousness throughout one's lifetime.

> *"We pray because we are programmed to pray. We think,*
> *because we have been programmed to think!"*
>
> — M Z

There are some adaptations as we proceed through life, but we still follow a natural tendency that go back to our original blueprint. Perhaps humans don't have the capacity to learn much beyond this prescribed formula. *(I have often wondered what it would take to get my dog to utter her first words.)*

The cybernetic world is not a lot different from you and me. We have been hard-programmed much like "ROM," Read Only Memory, and are forbidden from many other types of functions. *"I am because I think." "I think because I am."*

Genetic code locks in the certainty of our wiring. We do because we are compelled to do. We think because we are designed to think. Our consciousness is the dance of our neurons in an ordered movement.

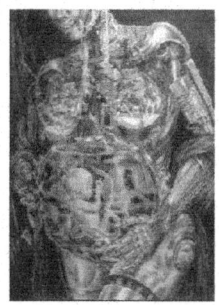

"The body is a great ark in a sea of randomness." —Matshona Dhliwayo

So, if our tendencies and programs run deep within us, it is likely that our wiring contains the very essence of our thoughts as well. And if we are not in control of these thoughts, we are sentenced to a reality of enslavement by something else.

This concept offers little encouragement of autonomy and fate of our eventual destiny. This idea supports the notion of a supreme being, and enforces a concept of divine intervention. This thought is scary at best!

I choose to view a slightly different reality. *"A reality where we are one with the creator." Not the pawn of eventuality!*

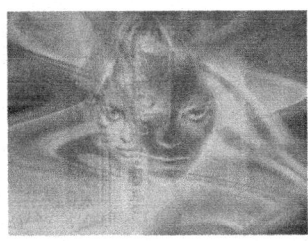

"God's hand is our hand. We are partnered in the process." —MZ

Perhaps we are shielded from certain realities, but faith tells me that this is part of a nurturing effort. We shelter our children from violence and harm's way, to protect and focus specific aspects of growth. Our children are appendages of ourselves, and also our best hope for the future. We too are the best promise for God. Interdependence is undeniable!

"The voices of control that beckons our instincts, are guided from a partnership of interdependence."

— M Z

We are developed from the seeds of others. In fact, we go back as many as 2,000 generations. The origins of man!

And from there, we may well go back several million more generations, as a result of breeding from ancient species.

All that is *"man,"* had millions of opportunities to mix together in a collective stew. Our DNA code makes up the human we know today. And that human, was type-cast from ancestors of every living creature on the face of the earth. *The human race is one big related family.*

From our historic mix, you could conclude that every life form on earth is a part of our family. We collectively are one and the same. We all arrived from the same origin, and hold a collective spirit through our DNA.

> *"We are the essence of life. Our order is the result*
> *of Universal development."*
>
> — M Z

As Carl Sagan once wrote, *"We are made of star stuff."* Billions of elements fabricated in a type of cosmic symphony. God by definition is all that is in the Universe. All that is in the Universe, including us, also defines "God."

If we are more like partners with God, perhaps we are components of a collective Godly spirit. God is us, and we are God. We are one! Perhaps it is "we" that judge ourselves, and also condemn ourselves.

So, if we are part of a collective spirit.., then all that we are, including our knowledge and consciousness, flows within our blood. God is within the fabric of our being! Our consciousness creates both our reality and our dreams. We are attached individually and most collectively.

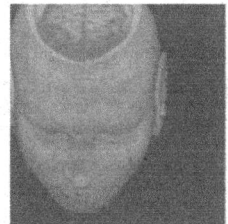

"Our prayers are self-healing. Our perspective is unique. Our relationship is undeniable." —MZ

As our collective can be described as a universal spirit, our thoughts are linked with the collective. We know what is right. We know our journey. *"We exist in the space of God."*

As we journey through our existence, we follow patterns from which we came. Our immediate ancestors may offer the best clues. We hold many reflections from the past, and this may point us in the direction of our origins. In a strange sense, we have lived before, through them. Our traits came from patterns in *"their"* thoughts. If they feared, then we fear. If they lived to survive, then we also must survive.

Spiritual Identity

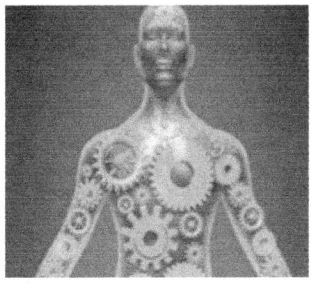

Each new discovery reinforces the mechanical nature of our material world. As we learn more about our biology and the world around us, we recognize the systematic programming in nature that defines our existence.

The question becomes, as we see more and more evidence of structure in nature, how could we expect to have free will? We are either *"mechanical beings"* running off of a biological script, or, we are *"spiritual beings"* that may be fabricating our biological construct. The world is either material/ mechanical, or it is not!

Science seems to be moving us in both directions at the same time. As we learn more about the genome, we see direct mechanical scripting in our biology, habits, and behavior. Our science demonstrates *"cause and effect,"* and that everything has a solid mathematical basis.

Until we get to the quantum world... We then see how mathematics and logic become irrelevant. How *"time,"* and *"cause and effect,"* are scrambled. How observation can affect outcomes. This should be a clue as to how *"consciousness"* may be dominating all that we experience. (*Experimental evidence is illustrated in pages 202 -208*)

While we accept the mathematical formula of our Universe, we also recognize the possibility that our mechanical Universe could be nothing more than a *"conscious construct."*

We *"will"* our world to appear as it does. We add discipline and structure to a contrived reality, as a type of hook or game that perpetuates its own fantasy. Like a movie or storyline, we continue to invent new chapters, as we build upon the already established script.

The game is always created within parameters established by the previous chapters. What fun would it be, if we had no rules or simply invented a world without consistency?

That is exactly what we do when we dream, or change the storyline. We usually keep a common thread of rules from our established construct. Perhaps we run trial episodes when we sleep, or daydream, testing thoughts against a backdrop of *"mechanical rules,"* established for our Universe.

If we are the ones who invent our Universe, and thus invent the mathematics and disciplines behind this Universe, (math, biology, etc...), then we also have the power to change the script and invent any reality we choose.

If we are convinced that we are not solely mechanical beings, and that the math behind the science, is to only give structure to a fabricated reality, then we must conclude *"consciousness"* is not derived from biology at all.

Rather, consciousness is transmitted from a source outside our biology. As earlier implied, the body may act more like a receiver, thus our thoughts may have origins independent of physical reality. As such, we hold the power of free will to construct any biology we want. Any material world we want.

The mechanics we observe may be nothing more than a grand illusion. We expect to see order, and so we see it. We expect our science to follow a script. And it does.

In this mechanical reality, our mind is stimulated by electrical patterns, and then turned off as *"delta brainwaves"* each night we sleep, much like a robot. But, we continue to process. When we rev-up the *"beta waves,"* we become acute and focused. Like an organ grinder churning a wheel.

The reality may be however, that we are mechanical beings with little free will, scripted only by outside forces from our soul. We direct the traffic, stimulate the activities, and utilize our imagination through our biological construct.

The soul may lead us down a rabbit hole of ever-increasing mathematics. Each new discovery finds more order and more structure, as we continue to crave the next milestone. We are taunted by the plausibility of a solid material world.

"Perhaps that is the real design."

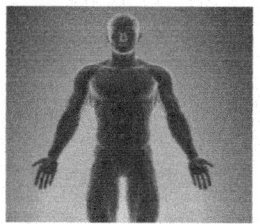

Does matter create thought?

This has been widely debated for centuries. We know from evidence of relativity (E=MC2), that energy and matter are most transferable. It is important to understand from where consciousness really emerges.

Traditional science has long assumed that consciousness is awakened by the interplay of neurons in the brain. Thus, when the brain no longer functions or *"brain dead,"* we are believed to be dead.

Current science is now revealing a substantial shift in this long-held assumption. Experiments have demonstrated there is no specific region in the brain where memory is stored. Instead, we find a whole network of neurons distributed throughout the body. Electrical activity can be stimulated by magnets and/or other energy impulses, and can be transmitted to outside mechanisms like artificial legs and limbs.

The human body is more of an electrical transmitter rather than a pure physical device.

We know that deep within the quantum, matter likely is electrical string energy, and thus its smallest natural state is energy. Energy is interchangeable into many forms. It can never be created or destroyed, but only transferred.

Experiments in *"After-death experiences,"* EKG's, etc.., have revealed strong evidence that we are electrical creatures. Thought is not centralized, but instead is distributed through-out the whole body as a network of electrical impulses.

It appears consciousness does not give rise from matter in the brain as once believed. *(Involuntary movements demonstrate this hypothesis.)* So, if thought is not derived from physical matter, it must be derived from a network of energy. And the origins of that network are clearly under great debate.

The *"Holographic Universe Hypothesis,"* has risen from the study of black holes. It concludes that information can never be created or destroyed, but instead, is stored on a two- dimensional space at an event horizon. This theory suggests we may actually be living on a two-dimensional Universe, and thus our 3D world is simply an illusion.

Noted scientists such as Leonard Susskind, Karl Pribram, Herman Verlinde, Gerard Hooft and many others, have generated great momentum in this field of study.

Based on what we know about the interpretive nature of our senses and the flexibility of our awareness, it is plausible that our consciousness is a mere projection filtered through our biological entity. When we die, our signal might be disrupted, however, the origin of the signal can never be destroyed. Any transmission continues forever.

The Human body is a conductor or generator of reality. Our dreamscape reveals the potential of conscious energy that is likely constructing and manufacturing our awareness.

Do we have Restrictive Amnesia?

Why do we dream, and why do we not always recall other aspects of our reality? Do we have restrictive Amnesia?

Here is a window into one of my specific dreams.

> *Its 4:00 a.m. in the morning as I wake from a deep sleep. I recall a conversation with my brother-in-law who is staying at our house, and not finding the right cereal in the pantry.*
>
> *We can find only Special K, and about 4 boxes. Well, I have never bought Special K and have no idea why we have it in the cabinets. He cannot seem to find anything he likes, and feels confined in a house where I assumed he had been comfortable vegging.*

As I try to explain where he can walk to find food, I can only remember what's outside the house I lived 40 years ago, or a Prairie Village home I lived 20 years later. As I am trying to awaken, I cannot seem to remember what is just outside my current house.

I try for several minutes, but I simply cannot remember where I am. I recognize everything inside the house, but cannot recall anything outside. I can't picture the street, or which direction to the nearest grocery. After a few minutes, it all begins to come back to me, but it didn't come easy.

Why was it so clear the details of my past environments, including his home out-of-state, yet I can't recall outside my own home, where I have lived the past 18 years?

There seems to be a symptom of short-term memory loss much like those of Alzheimer patients. They often remember the past, but are confused in the present. *Perhaps this is symptomatic of something else?* Time and place have no meaning in our sleep, and this distortion is the natural state of our subconscious.

On that morning of my twilight recollection, other places had as much relevance as the current. Not only do the scenes and actors change, but my own persona also changes. This is most enlightening as to how I am moved in time.

In this story, I can remember directions in alternative time frames, but not necessarily the current one. This appears to be a clue that our timeline is most fragile. *Perhaps our current time-frame is not necessarily the relevant one.*

Current reality may not be as relevant as we think it is! From a physiology standpoint, *"why would short term memory be any different than long term memory."* It shouldn't be! Yet, this seems to be a common symptom of Alzheimers.

Research suggests that this condition generates a subtle degeneration in the hippocampus synaptic region. There is no distinguishable physiological difference between long and short-term memory. If a region is impaired, it should affect long-term memory as well, but that is not what is observed.

Long-term memory has a curious way of re-establishing itself. Often, we have an easier time recalling distant memories. And those memories can be as vivid and real as the present.

THE SUBCONSCIOUS

An example of mental gymnastics is the fact that the human brain demonstrates both conscious and subconscious reality.

Scientists have revealed that 85 percent of brain function is within the subconscious realm. Automatic responses control heart rate, blood pressure, adrenal functions, and all cellular activity. Our bodies self-heal, by the division and replacement of cells that make up our existence. We never have to think much about a physical injury, because this automatic self-healing process operates in the background a bit like "magic."

Our neurons are organized in phases of electrical charges that exhibit regular cycles of brainwave activity. This activity directs the functionality of our heart, and all bodily functions, as we move through regular cycles. We exist as a machine that continues to tick whether we take control of it or not.

Automated responses are regulated by the subconscious mind, the same mind where dreams and intuition originate. We seem to have awareness outside of consciousness, and that deepened awareness is critical for our survival.

Scientists have shown that "consciousness" is stimulated at the tip of our frontal lobe. The subconscious is stimulated by the lower regions of the sub cortex, and is always running actively in the background. The subconscious mind dictates our dreams, and also all "daydreaming" activities.

Research using electroencephalogram or (EEG monitors), show that our brainwaves follow four very distinctive electrical patterns.

1. **Beta waves,** are rapid frequencies "14 to 20" cycles per minute, and is mostly recognized as our "consciousness."

   However, most of our brain activity resides in the subconscious realm where we see the following cycles;

2. **Alpha waves,** "7 to 14" cycles per minute, occur during daydreaming and automatic mental functions like walking. It is estimated that 50 percent of our brain activity is in this stage.

3. **Theta waves,** only exhibit "4 to 7" cycles per minute. This describes the next deeper level where we enter a state of meditation. It is believed that this is where memories are stored.

4. **Delta waves,** are characterized by "0 to 4" cycles per minute, and describes a very deep sleep. It is believed that consciousness is absent as a natural mechanism for body and cellular regeneration.

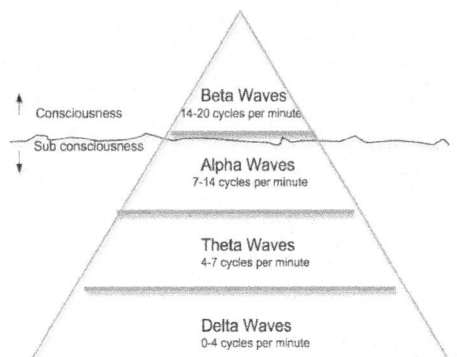

85% of all brain power is in the subconscious

During sleep, we also enter four phases as it relates to both rapid eye movement (REM), and brain activity.

1. **Light Sleep** – With limited eye movement is usually measured in the theta wave range.

2. **Regular Sleep** – Also has limited eye movement, but in a much deeper theta stage. It's estimated we spend 50% of our sleeping hours here.

3. **Deep Sleep** – Also describes limited eye movement, but we fall into a delta realm. No dreaming, and completely out of consciousness as deemed necessary for cellular growth.

4. **REM Sleep** (Rapid Eye Movement) - We move into a dream state with brain activity equivalent to our beta "waking" phase. Here we experience brain activity independent of conscious reality.

As we sleep, we move through several cycles of all four stages. It remains unknown why we enter these sleep stages, or what ultimate benefit that our dreams may represent.

We don't necessarily need to be asleep to tap the energy of our subconscious. We do it regularly and more frequently than normal waking consciousness. We have learned a variety of functions, such as walking, talking, twitching etc.., and we execute these acts most subconsciously. All that we do is designed and visualized before we do it. So, it is *"thought,"* that actually generates this reality.

It has been shown that given a battle between the conscious mind and the subconscious, the subconscious is far more powerful and usually wins.

In battling addictions, one can make a conscious effort to do a certain task such as "quit smoking" yet the subconscious is more dominant. Another example might be dieting, where you "will" yourself not to eat, but your subconscious usually overpowers your will. It takes strict and dedicated training to overcome these most powerful urges.

Hypnotism has proven that the power of suggestion can influence behavior by tapping strength from the subconscious. A qualified hypnotist can place subjects into a deep trance and influence incredible suggestions. The subject may appear relaxed and awake, but is actually very suggestible to outside commands.

Physiologically, the eyes take on a blank stare as if seeing a world that does not exist. Much like a jump start into a REM sleep, a person may see and do things outside of conscious control. Cluck like a chicken, walk in circles, bathe on a beach, or assume a new identity. All while the hypnotist is in control and making the suggestions.

It is often claimed that one would not do acts of violence, if called to do so. That hypnosis is safe and beneficial. But this could remain the subject of some debate. Much like the "Manchurian Candidate," one could be compelled to do all kinds of unthinkable acts.

More commonly, one can form attitudes and opinions that are persuaded by others. The field of advertising and politics has demonstrated this example. We have seen many forms of social hypnosis. Some might call it "brain washing." But the mere fact that we can be brainwashed at all, demonstrates the susceptibility of our psyche.

So, do we have free will?

If others can influence our subconscious, and that subconscious becomes our invented reality, are we regularly being manipulated by forces outside of our control?

And if others can influence our subconscious, do we also play a part in influencing that reality?

It is very clear that the subconscious operates from an alternative perspective from conscious reality. Every night we experience this when we sleep.

Subconscious awareness that controls our intuition, instincts, and regulated body functions, could also be described as a background programming. Like, perhaps the function of our soul.

We receive regular ongoing directives from outside forces everyday. We independently shape our subconscious.

Hypnotists claim that we often hypnotize ourselves. And that is the real secret to their magic. The brain sees what it wants to see. We build a world around that.

We can look directly at a cup of water and never see it. No matter how hard we look, our brain omits the image. This can be either self-induced or introduced by another into the subconscious.

"Hocus Pocus"

A hypnotized individual might see a blue sky and sunshine, although they may actually be in a dark room and lying on a bed. The experience is very real, and often the same as described in our dream state.

When shaving my face each morning, I notice I always start on the right side, and move in a horizontal stroke to the left. I always place my first shoe on the right. My bowel movement is always 7:00 a.m. sharp, on central time.

I have a cookie jar in the kitchen, and every time I take a cookie, I think of my distant "Uncle Jim." So strange is this association that I actually decided one day, to place a label on the inside of the Jar with his name on it.

Habits appear to be another word for programming. And such programming resides deep in our subconscious. There seems to be an association between the subconscious and the soul. The soul also appears to be a kind of programming, or *"directive,"* and always operating in the background of our consciousness.

Why do we have both conscious and subconscious experiences?

For years, we have tried to understand the context of our living experiences. This includes one third of our life in the subconscious reality of sleep.

In waking hours, we spend 85% of our brain activity in the automatic functions of theta waves, "daydreaming" and "automatic processes." Our conscious activities describe only a small portion of who we actually are.

The Art of Positive Thinking

We seem to have the ability to alter and correct our thought patterns by methods of self-hypnosis and meditation. We hold the power to influence our attitudes and perceptions within our own environment.

It has been shown that positive thinking can modify reality, and encourage motivated behavior. Motivation plays a key role in success and your will to succeed. **Positive thinking is not about fooling yourself, but rather viewing a different side of reality.**

"Positive thinking is not to distract from truth, but to focus attention on functional truths often obscured."

—HENRI MATISSE

Biofeedback loops have been shown effective in modifying desired behavior. We can manipulate our thoughts, and generate a new version of practical reality. The *"placebo effect,"* has been proven to influence our physical anatomy, and actually modify the functions of our physical body. We know stress has a big impact on physical health.

Hypnotic time distortion / The bend of reality

Time distortion is a very real component of hypnosis. When the mind drifts into autopilot as characterized by alpha waves, we experience time passing very quickly and abstractly. As we fall deeper into stages of theta waves or *"sleep,"* time can appear to progress at the snap of a finger.

"Have you ever fallen asleep at night, and suddenly it was morning? Time in the dream phase has no relevance at all."

In the Womb

Scientists have determined that we begin developing our subconscious about 6-8 weeks in the womb. We seem to have a fundamental will to be born, and we are baited by stimuli outside the womb.

Are babies conscious?

The cortex, the epicenter of human consciousness, start to form in about the sixth month. Neuroscientists speculate that within the later stages of pregnancy, the fetus is familiar with the sound of its mother's voice, and may already be learning language. It is believed that babies initially develop in a delta state, and then from 5-9 months, move progressively to the theta state of brain activity.

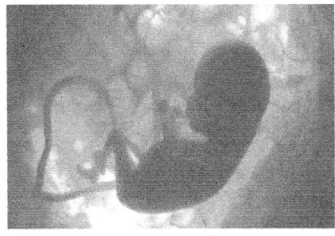

Ongoing Programming

As we drift from consciousness, we build small mind scripts or short *"program triggers."* This causes the brain to move into an auto pilot mode. Mind scripts incorporate old memories with current experience and builds automatic triggers. By implementing time distortion, one can access deeper stored memories.

When I was in school, I remember sitting in math class and being totally bored. Time crept along very slowly, as the second hand on the clock seemed to tick slower and slower. Each minute felt like hours.

As I spend many hours working on creative endeavors such as music, time usually passes in a snap. Many of my musical skills have been relegated to automatic memory responses of chords and scales. Before I know it, several hours have passed. Again, time has no meaning.

There are people who can calculate mathematics in an instant mentally. There are fantastically successful baseball players, who experience the ball coming toward them much slower than others. High-speed readers, who read over 2,000 words per minute, experience a sense of time distortion as information flashes through their mind in seconds.

As Einstein pointed out, time flows at different rates for each person. Some people have experienced their entire life flash before their eyes, in a matter of seconds prior to sudden- death experience. Dream researchers have recognized that a one-minute dream can be experienced as hours. Our thoughts have a time frame all their own.

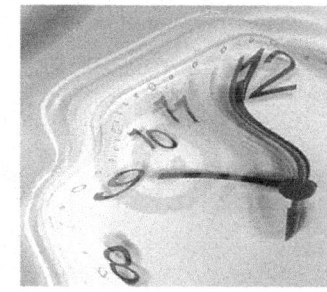

A form of time dilation

Dream Encroachment

An example of when dreams overlap the lines of reality can be illustrated in these personal dream experiences.

"It was late one night when I had a dream about a tiger pacing around, and then attacking a young boy. I was scared, and tried to lure the tiger away to save the child. But it was too late, and it was horrific. I then tried to clean up the grounds as to not spook others watching close by."

The next morning in my waking hours, I looked on Facebook, and sure enough, another person had posted a tiger attack on a child. I had not read such an article at any time in recent memory. The thought of a tiger mauling someone had not occurred to me. If ever! But for some reason, that one night after my dream, I was holding a tangible article that reflected what I dreamed about the night before. It was a slightly different story, but relevant in so many ways. How did this rare and unlikely dream precede a rare article found the next morning? The mystery continues.

In another example, *"I had dreamed of an argument with my son. Both went away mad. As I was driving away, I got a call from a woman I believed to be a nurse. "Mr Zembrowski? Yes, I replied. "Brian has just passed away." How did it happen? "He took his life." In the dream, I experienced a complete melt down throwing papers and trashing the walls.*

The next morning in the Kansas City Star, I read an article about a boy who ran away from home and took his life. Police said it was an apparent suicide. I don't recall ever reading an article like that ever before."

In a final example, *"I am traveling in a plane coasting over mountains somewhere in South America. The pilot gives me the controls and I continue to fly for quite some time. The pilot described to me, that the longer one fly's, the greater chance for an accident. I discussed how careful I would be, and continued to test my soaring ability.*

The very next day, I witnessed a Facebook blog about a man and his funeral in Mississippi. He had died in a plane crash that took the life of both himself and his instructor. I am still trying to recall his name, but he was from Central America. I don't often dream of flying in a private plane, and I almost never see a blurb about a crashed plane."

Coincidence or is there a connection?

Many people have claimed that events often happen in 3s... There appears to be some kind of mathematical formula that rules our events. Thus, the rise of astrology and numerology.

More and more, I have been gaining the feeling that things don't just happen. Why a car suddenly pulls out on me when trying to back out, or why traffic lights never match the odds of my travel path.

Dreams often relate to matters that have not necessarily happened yet. Time has no relevance there. Unconscious dreams tend to overlap and ferret out ideas experienced in the conscious world. Over and over, we have described how time is irrelevant in our dream-state, but in our waking, we are conditioning for what we might imagine next.

These three examples provoke the idea that, we are creating dreams, and the ideas that carry them out. Could we also be creating our waking state, and writing scripts of what we are next to pursue?

Before we jump off a curb, we are imagining it. Before we decide to eat, we are visualizing it. Before we wake, are we creating it? This teases further evidence that we may be creating our reality.

The Dreamscape

Through interpretation of dreams, I have come to several unique conclusions. One is that we dream beyond just black and white. In fact, we dream in multi-colors as demonstrated by the fact I can describe specific colors without mistake. Therefore, it is the brain that interprets colors, and not the cones of the eye.

The second observation is that we do in fact have multiple dreams over the same fictitious episodes. I've experienced the same dreams over and over, of events and landscapes that I know to be false. A vision of a downtown riverfront keeps reoccurring without any basis in fact. Could this mean we are inventing our dreams? And if so, are we also creating a consistent storyline?

A third observation is that *"I am, and I always was."* My earliest memories highlight a certain consistency of thought pattern. I have always had an internal dialogue with myself, and believe I did even prior to my birth.

This leads to a conclusion that I am somewhat in control of my own Universe. My Universe is based on my reality and vantage, much like the perspective of time itself.

JOURNEY THROUGH TIME

It is 8:00am in the morning as I jump out of bed in a Tudor styled home that seems to have a lingering aura all its own.

I look under my bed next to the stuffed tiger animal, and find the Indian moccasins I have become so fond of. GI-Joe is still lying on its side where I left it.

Running down the stairs, I am excited to see Grandma and Grandpa ready to energize my special day. Yes, for today it's my birthday, and I am all of 6 years old.

The day begins with early presents and a fun day planned, birthday guests arriving within the hour. The regular lunch team from school arrives and I am the center of the day's activities.

Spin-the-bottle, pin-the-tail-on-the-donkey, and tumbling down the front yard. It was all about being silly.

As I shift my position in bed, I begin to see myself sitting in the principal's office and waiting for Wane T. Snyder to render judgment for some kind of schoolyard infraction.

Mostly nervous and scared, I then shift to sitting in a high- chair eating from the blue box of Gerber. The tasty oatmeal paste dribbling down my chin, as for the first time I was in control of my own eating, and loved every minute of it.

Flash forward to waking up at 3:00am in the morning with a blue alarm clock flickering reminiscent of the vinyl leather couch and stereo clock at Park 25 Apartments in Lawrence.

Time dilation seems to be happening as I lay still in my bed in Overland Park. A full 56 years has passed, yet I continue to dredge up experiences and episodes while I try to allow my mind to rest.

3:45 a.m., I go back to sleep again. A flashing blue light conjures up a memory of a streetscape closed on the plaza, some 12 years before.

As I fall into a deeper and deeper sleep, I am walking along a street with a river front park across the road. I can see it is downtown Kansas City, but has no resemblance to buildings there today. A carnival is happening, yet for some reason I can't go. Hotels and buildings line the street, where suddenly I find myself in Cincinnati, living in a strange Tudor house once again.

It seems I am free to fly wherever I want. Enter any dream, and remember any time. *And not all are my own!*

The act of being human offers unlimited conscious flexibility and a large degree of mental elasticity. Forward and backwards. Faster and slower. Timeless and pre-conscious. I move from one place to another often on stimulation from my current world.

Language is transmitted through feelings and emotions. And those feelings and emotions seem to transcend the concept of personal linear time.

Drift of Social Reality

Another example of movement through time, relates to the drift of society in the actual physical world itself.

In the summer 2011, I published a genealogy book, compiling information that I had related to my family genealogy and my past.

In Chapter One of the "Zembrowsky Genealogy," I described the history of Castle Garden and my family's entry into the United States via New York. Jews of eastern European descent, settled in the lower eastside of Manhattan between Hester and Delancey Street. This area became known as a Jewish historical Mecca, around the turn of the century, as thousands settled to maintain their Yiddish heritage there.

Much of American Jewish culture was launched from this unique area. This later produced Jewish theater, Vaudeville, Hollywood, Garment, and Jewelry industries, Labor Unions, Financial institutions and so much more.

As time marched on, many of the WWII generation children, moved out of the area and into the suburbs, where the likes of Reform Judaism flourished.

During my earlier childhood in the 1960s, I remember visiting this historic area of Delancey street, and amazed by the old- world Jews still living there. In retrospect, this area must have represented the culture of the newest immigrants from the WWII era. Now some 20-30 years later, there were Jews still living an existence in this old-world community.

As I returned to the area in the late 1990s with my wife, I realized a sizable group living as before. One observation however was, *"Wow these people looked old."*

In reality, they were, old. They were the elderly remnants of WWII immigrants that raised children who had moved out of the area. This was what was left from the last wave of immigration. After WWII, most Jews had already migrated, and most new immigrants were moving to Israel. The 1990s represented a time of aging immigrants, locked in a former culture characterized by a most identifiable district.

Now recently in 2014, *(just about 20 years later)*, I returned to the area and found another surprise. I walked and walked the district bordered by Houston Street on the north, and Hester to the south. Yet, I saw not one Hebrew sign, not one Yiddish storefront. Instead, I saw Chinese writing everywhere as if it were an expansion of China-Town.

The truth was that I was actually in China-Town. It expanded over the Italian and Jewish East-Side neighborhoods, now with recent Chinese immigrants.

Reality struck me that those old Jewish immigrants from the WWII era, like my own parents, were now all dead. There has been little Jewish immigration for 60 years, and that once relevant and impactful Jewish ghetto, is now gone.

Like a weird description of a drive through Kansas City in the next chapter, all neighborhoods have shifted and changed.

So too has the landscape of the lower New York East Side.

Populations will ebb and flow, and none more evident than the Jewish community that is in a regular state of movement and flux. The inspirational center for so many great Americans, can now hardly find its own origins.

The buildings are all there. Some rehabbed and improved into bars and art studios. The ghost of the Jewish people is all that is left in both Eastern Europe, and on the East-Side shores of Manhattan.

In its turn-of-the-century heyday, the Lower East-Side was home to a flourishing Jewish community of Germans, Eastern Europeans, Russians, and Greeks. They lived in cramped tenements and peddled pushcarts or toiled in the garment industry for a living. They were the agitators for social reform, establishing synagogues, community centers, Yiddish theater, newspapers, and Zionist activities. Now just a fade in history, of what once was.

Brave New World

Recently, I began to reflect on how much my own world has changed over time. Many relationships that once were, have moved on, and disbursed throughout the country. Curiously, without a compelling need to return to their roots.

As I journey through life, I have always felt a draw to return to a center. Unfortunately, many of the lives and faces have evaporated into a kind of surreal abyss. Memories have faded into a distorted backdrop of what was.

Times and people change over time, and new relationships and experiences nurture an ominous feeling of paralysis. Today, I see a more robotic world in all aspects of existence. Technology has ruled the habits and minds of the populous, while encouraging a more apathetic existence.

There appears to be less substance in a world that often looks like everything else. A strange drift into more of an observer than a participant!

Pursuing this logic, one could ask the question *"am I the same person I once was?" "Am I connected in the same way?"* And if the world is a stage more like that of window dressing, *"am* I limited as only an *observer?"* *"Am I still real or alive?"*

> *"The world's a stage, and all the men and women merely players... They have their exits and their entrances. One man in his time plays many parts."*
>
> —WILLIAM SHAKESPEARE

There appears to be a gradual shift from substance to irrelevance. A bond that once cemented my being is now more fragmented and obscured. *"A rich origin is forever altered, and then diluted through the process of time."*

If I compare the being I once was 15 years ago, with who I am today, the glue of my spirit has been substantially modified. ***"For sure, all my cells have been replaced by now!"***

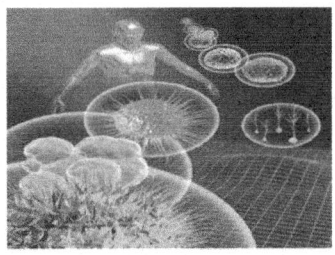

It seems that a gradual defragmentation of spirit also occurs, shaping a new entity. The spirit that once was, has been altered, replaced, or perhaps morphed into a new phase of reality.

It could be argued that I am now dead, but not yet aware.

"Am I an observer or participant?" "Am I affecting others?" "Are they affecting me?" "Am I the same force that once was, as I age with diminished eyesight, and physical faculties?"

Are we living a new drama today, with one foot in this world, while trying to maintain a leg in the past? Perhaps this is how the spirit is supposed to be. Always changing and experiencing fresh observations! Yet, the more observations obtained, the more surreal and unconnected from the original experience.

A Floating Spirit

In another example of a dream, I was floating like a spirit. My father whispered to me, "It's not your fault that your house is getting destroyed." (Something about pipes bursting on the first floor below.)

I am asleep lying upstairs in a bed and not "supposed" to be awake. Was I dead? It is interesting, that I describe myself in this conversation as "you." Who is narrating this story? Is it me or someone else?

My father came to tell me that it was OK that I am not awake. He guides me down the stairs where chunks of landing had been taken out. The landing is green and black with an oak midpoint, in a house I assumed was 3545 Paseo. (I noticed that the address chosen was my father's old home.) It was an older house with a smallish dark living room. It had stucco walls, and a skylight overlooking the driveway just left of the staircase.

It is not my fault that spirits were destroying the house. I listened intently and heard oohing sounds with very distant voices. When I tried to interact, one rose up and startled me.

I turned away and I saw another, and another. I became so agitated, that I began to bounce around and shout back at all these spirits I had encountered.

I noticed that my bouncing was like flying also like a spirit.

(I guess I was a spirit.) I had the company of my father with me, and we together were trying to hold on to our house.

I even yelped in my sleep that woke my wife in bed.

My father's presence was with me. The memories had little reflection of accurate times, as I experience characters across generations. This episode was just as relevant as anything currently in my head. Yet, it seemed all too familiar.

If hypnosis can bring back old stored memories, then how does it distinguish between old stored memories in my mind, and those mental images I fabricate in my head at night?

Can hypnosis bring back thoughts and ideas I form in REM sleep? I created these episodes in my head that seem real at the time. Most people forget their dreams, but can those dreams also be resurrected?

A strange question arises; are these recollections even mine? Are these my fabrications, or someone else's altogether?

In Summary,

The dream I experienced in the house with my brother-in-law, demonstrates that we have selective memory. We can shield many things from our regular reality. What else might we be shielding?

Reliving life as a 6-year-old, and then again at age 52, demonstrates a flexibility of perspective, and how we can invent any reality we choose through our consciousness.

Colors and perceptions are not the result of tools of the body, but instead are fabricated as a construct in our minds. We create themes and similarity of character, and we always narrate from a familiar voice.

The previous three examples, where reality crossed over from dreams and re-emerged in life, may demonstrate how reality can be affected by our dreams. Time association gets confused as we only believe we perceive the order of events.

That order, can be volatile as we actually dream both before and after we experience. Our dreams can be a premonition, or it can also be a fabrication from the past.

Lastly, as I fly like a spirit, I question whether these thoughts are even mine at all. Am I taking a persona of another entity entirely? Am I seeing visions from another time and place, or from someone else's perspective?

I find little distinction between the dreamscape and current reality. All seem to be ongoing and regular cycles of the mind.

Time Marches On

As described earlier, much of our reality is reflected from that of others. When someone dies, that reflection ceases. The make-up of one's character has been altered as a result of *"death by reflection."* From that day forward, one absorbs a concept of what was, and builds an everlasting impression of the deceased. *"The living generates their own interpretation of the person."*

When we die, we leave the world a different place from where we began. Through the march of history, our reality now includes new fashions, heroes, technology, attitudes, and political will.

Walking through life we try to resurrect the ghost, but the ghost continues to fade, and reality continues to move on. 2015 resembles nothing of 1957, and I am sure that in the span of a lifetime, more and more becomes unrecognizable.

The voices of the past become silenced, and the noise of the current, is often shrill and brash. And in that brashness, little seems to match the original mission of the journey.

A case can be made, that 15 years ago matching a death,

I perhaps realized a partial death as well. Once in the background of parental influences that shared in joys and sorrow, today, that echo rings hollow and reflective of a diminishing reality.

"Without the benefit of relationships, I can't imagine living life in isolated solitaire."

—MZ

The other night I slept, and experienced a whole lifetime of conversations, places, and activities. Recollections that were mundane, sometimes adventurous, and certainly most real at the time.

As I woke, I rejected my return to this current place and time. For hours, I tried to recall the actions of my dreams, and questioned which place I truly belonged.

I felt a compelling need to walk the streets of neighborhoods that once were. And as I did, I reflected on what I see now, and how it fit into this new scheme. A thought occurred, that perhaps I have already been dead, walking through a tunnel of new reality.

I began to think about the movement of time, and if I were to bring someone back 50 years later, how that person might experience today. If my own grandfather who died in 1959 were suddenly catapulted to 2015, he would know no one. He would vaguely recognize the technology, and would have little understanding of the political and social will of the time. The evils of Nazi Germany still fresh on his mind.

If we are who we're projected against, then my grandfather would be truly in a foreign land. Fighting to discover his own morals and ideals, while meandering in a strange and altered world. This would represent the ultimate search of, *"who I am,"* in a world moved in time and space.

Ghost of Society

As we have described throughout this book, culture affects society and imbeds its own personality into its community.

That community becomes your living reality and plants the goals, morals, and inspiration of the individual. A person grows up with a sense of community, and develops a spiritual awareness around what has been conditioned through *his* or *her* elders.

Such identity creates a living link to the Universe and is responsible for the formulation of your soul. As community spirit grows and wanes, the components of your being may evaporate through time. Once real and impactful, it can be diluted to nothing more than dreams or a guiding direction for your views, attitudes, and awareness.

This very subject is the basis for a community spirit that can move and adapt with the flow of nature. The point is, that we are not necessarily one, but the product of thousands of cultural influences that make up our being. These same cultural influences can touch many lives, and affect many identities. Each identity is never alone but part of a collective. That collective may best describe the concept of God.

Influences are not always physical but can also be spiritual in nature. We don't necessarily need to live on earth, or be a physical being in order to experience reality. That is why we can cross the lines of living and dead, past or present. This describes the wide scope of the human entity, and our elastic concept of our life and time.

DYNAMICS OF THE SOUL

Part C

Dynamics of the Soul

Before we explore the concept of time and soulful evolution, we should better understand the relationship between "time and matter," and how it "might" affect the flow of conscious energy. Assuming that soulful migration is a natural process in our Universe, I will describe how this relationship *"might"* work.

Time is measured as an observation or (relationship) to an event! Various vantage points will measure the same event, at a slightly different time. Thus, time is *"variable"* with respect to location.

Time is represented by the separation of matter. The movement of each individual particle is affected by the tug of various forces. Gravity then plays a key role on the drag and pull of energy, as matter moves from one point to another.

Being farther from an event, puts you ahead of the time curve, and technically allows you to observe an event that happened in the past. All observation arrives after the fact, because it takes time for light to travel to your location. Therefore, each observation is always in the past, much like that of a distant star.

Moving farther from an event slows your ability to receive the observation. *(This assumes the observation is sight perceived.) The event lags into the past.* By contrast, your relationship actually moves into the future.

In theory, by moving away, you allow an event to pass more slowly *(delaying receipt,)* and thus slowing time.

When moving *in the same direction of an event,* you receive the observation more quickly. This shortens any time lag, and moves your position closer to the event. Relative time passes sooner, diminishing the lag between past and present. Your coordinates have moved backward in time as you approach its origin.

There appears to be a point of finite past, as your coordinates are one and the same with an event. But even at the point of origination, your consciousness requires time to disseminate information. That information adds additional dimensionality.

As the quantum world has demonstrated, consciousness itself will affect the observation. This calls into question whether an event ever took place or not. You can only "believe" you are interacting at any given point. There is a conscious element in constructing the reality of any event. *(If a tree falls, and no one observed it, did it happen?)*

I suppose one could go back further in time, by observing the components used in creating the event. In other words, observing "pre-event" motion of matter. But that does not address the consciousness required in fabricating the act.

The only way to go back in time "pre-event," is to create a conscious re-construction. Time, as we know it does not exist prior to the event, and that eerily describes the "Big Bang."

In our physical Universe, even the slightest shift in direction would skew the components that make up the event. All components of an event (matter,) or any deviation in position would change each independent relationship. Time is affected on the most minute level, including each particle involved.

If we were to observe the motion of pre-event molecules, those components would be arriving from different origins.

No matter where you are in point and time, your relationship would be skewed with respect to those components. Time is flexible by each individual relationship of matter.

So, can you travel back to pre-event time? The answer is no, because time at its most minute level is always relative to what it is measured against. Time is completely flexible and skewed by each position in time and space. There is never a precise definition of time.

"Time has no relevance forward or backward!" It all exists in the now!

Speed of motion is another factor, as well as direction from the event. Because all observation arrives at different rates and times, our sensory would receive the information at different intervals.

"A sound of thunder lags behind the light that already flashed, and so on..."

One problem is, that Albert Einstein demonstrated that the speed of light is finite, and thus one cannot move faster than light. But light can be slowed, and that alone will create a dynamic passage of events.

Sound is 820,000 times slower than light, depending on the medium that conducts it. Speed of light is also variable by what conducts its signal as well. This would account for any changes in its fixed speed. *(Perhaps exceeding the speed of light is nothing more than a dimensional transfer.)*

Smell and taste impulses move yet slower through neural receptors. *"ESP,"* or other methods of transcendental travel, may actually move information faster than light, as observed from quantum particle correlation.

Perhaps we will find dimensional bridges that can enhance, or take shortcuts through the natural motion of our Universe. And that opens the door to yet new dimensional possibilities.

All information arrives at specific points in space-time at very different arrival points. The reality of any action would stretch dramatically based on each variable receiving it. We live in all kinds of bubbles and distortions. Our awareness is skewed by the symphony of impressions that move through the Universe.

Time and Gravity

As we recognize the *"elasticity"* of time from relative vantage points, and how gravity bends and stretches our Universe, we can see how dynamic the Universe really is. Speed is also a factor in the dissemination of information.

We know the Universe is not consistent, and that matter is often clustered and unbalanced from what we might expect from the tugs of gravity. This suggests many dynamic possibilities.

Gravitational forces create bubbles and distortions throughout space-time. There are weak forces, and more concentrated forces that create various densities of time and matter. Distance is the measure*ment of "speed over* time," and thus both speed and time are variable, as one travels through forces in nature.

Matter moves through *"ripples and distortions"* as it travels through the cosmos. Time is reflected by its relationship with particle separation. So, as matter and energy alter, so does time.

Entropy then rules the direction of our Universe. As its natural state of disorder progresses, the reliability of time and any cosmic direction becomes increasingly more complicated.

By using a simple yardstick to measure distances throughout the Universe, the yardstick would be unreliable. Gravitational forces would either stretch or compress each measurement from region to region.

Everything has gravitational attraction that plays on everything else. Every molecule has an altering affect that skews the passage of time. The strong and weak force of atoms further affects the movement of these particles.

As the Universe is always in motion, we experience micro-distortions on a second-by-second basis here on earth. These distortions may appear so *slight as to go undetected,* but is uniquely skewed at every point of reference.

Wherever there are larger gravitational variations, you would expect larger time distortions. Each region is affected by its own molecular flow. Time distortion on earth is commonly less volatile than more unstable regions of space. Thus, time flows erratically, near unstable regions like black holes.

The chemical firings of our neurons have a direct correlation with our physical Universe affected by gravity. The fabric of space-time affects molecular structures, and this correlation directly affects our neurons and ultimately our consciousness.

Each neuron firing projects its own unique signature. It is plausible that the flow of such energy is projected through a kind of *"data stream,"* in a unique and personal sequence.

This may prove to project our *"thoughts"* and our genetic awareness.

Because space-time is flexible, reality may actually follow many alternate variations at once. Particularly in view that "cause and effect" may be interchangeable. A person's conscious make-up, may actually cross over several planes, and bind several realities from a common source.

Additionally, you might not be alone in your unique identity, as this data stream regularly merges with other forms of consciousness. *"A kind of interplay of evolution and soul."*

As we learn more about the *electro-magnetic* nature of our brain, and how it affects thought processes, we have seen how magnets and electrical stimuli affect our consciousness. Various ionic charges will affect brain activity, our memory, and our intuition.

Waves or ripples of matter run through the cosmos like flows of a stream. Pushed by gravitational forces, it flows into channels of matter and energy causing rivers of time variation. Such flows may separate and flow together again, creating a type of delta or *(vortex)* of time and energy.

"Vortexes may exist on earth at multiple places, joining together the flow of conscious energy ("souls,") from a variety of recent journeys."

Souls are naturally guided by the cosmic direction of their flow, and meet at junctures of alternate realities. Those sensitive to these energy patterns, can be aware of ancient stimuli such as smells, laughs, sounds, etc, that all bond together the spiritual senses.

"Have you ever extracted a complete character from mannerisms, body language or human emissions? Most people do and the results are unbelievably accurate."

Each current is unique and may meet at substantially different junctures in time and space. Spiritual flow may arrive from completely different origins, and are interconnected through variations of cosmic attraction.

"Thought energy is confined to closer time frames. Like waves on an ocean, moderate motion is more common than the arc of a title wave."

Larger gravitational disparities produce larger time distortions. Therefore, time deviation and its spiritual flow, are generally within tighter time frames. *"Give or take a few hundred years."*

Vaster time frames and its correlated energy would hide behind a more recent past. Longer time spans would tend to shadow behind the more recent, thus blending and merging together a common spirit.

"You might be aware of influences of several lifetimes past, but your most vivid perceptions are that of a most recent awareness."

This gives support to the fact that our most recent ancestors may offer the best clues to our past. Our recent spiritual linage is most relevant to our present. This also works similar to the evolution of our DNA.

Our living experience builds on a compilation of ancestral forces that regulate our time and place. Each movement opens new gateways, and carves new living adventures. We are the result of attractive forces, and an example of our great historic journeys.

Memory Drive

In the winter of 2007, I found myself taking a drive through the neighborhoods of Kansas City, looking for a strange sense of inner self. My entire existence has been nothing more than a walk through the time and places that have defined my being.

As I drove through older sections of town, I realized that nothing lasts forever. The area that once was the driving force of my experience growing up, is now only a shadowy shell of its former self.

As I drive down *"Holmes Road"* in Kansas City, I came across the former Jewish Community Center. This Center built to reflect the roots of Eastern European immigrants, had a kind of Middle Eastern-Israeli looking architecture.

My earliest recollections of that time, were simply avoiding the Yiddish older ladies immersed in theater and B'nai B'rith, and taking a class or two from a hip young *"fashion nut,"* destined to recreate his place on a kibbutz in Israel. *"Folk music, Hava Nagila, and Israel or bust!"*

Today, as I continued this journey, I witness only a boarded building, with tangled weeds infesting the rock wall structure. No signs of life! As if I were seeing an aftermath of nuclear fallout.

Across the way sat old dilapidated houses, with rusted out pick-up trucks parked in the front yard. No sign of Jewish life what-so-ever. Of course, most Jews had migrated to Johnson County where it was clear each generation had moved regularly from somewhere else. *(Can we say wandering?)*

As I furthered my journey, I drove past the demolished Temple B'nai Jehudah at 69th and Holmes, where now sits a completely unrecognizable structure. Just like the Eastern Europeans of today, and the immigrants of lower Manhattan, little to no signs remain.

B'nai Jehudah Temple "left," corner of Linwood Boulevard & Flora, was occupied in 1908, and was the third temple to be used by this Jewish congregation. On the "Right," the 4th "snow coned" temple built 1967.Now only for the history books...

As I'm driving down Pennsylvania Avenue, I recall riding my bike through *"Rooster Island"* and always running from the Americans. It was a shoot-out starting from the Shea's front porch, where both of our fathers were veterans of the war.

My father was only a lowly sergeant, and the Shea's father was of course the more important Captain. It seemed that I was always the one playing the role of the Germans, getting shot at and on the run. I kept getting caught up in this strange role reversal. The only Jewish kid in the neighborhood, yet always forced to be the German. I lost every battle including a battle for identity. I was forced to think like a German.

Somehow, it felt familiar...

I remembered the Boy Scout troop with the secret dark rooms at the Country Club Christian Church. I expected a bolt of lightning to strike me at any moment from an angry God!

I passed through the short cuts between garages where I stumbled upon several civil war bullets and old pottery. It seemed that history passed right through my back yard here.

The strangest feeling of all was that this recent trip down memory lane was like *"a joy ride chasing my soul."* There is a spiritual tug-of-war going on. Not necessarily of the religious aspect of my life, but rather an accumulation of experiences that included buildings, landscapes, fears, hopes & dreams, and visions from my past.

As I'm driving down the elm-lined boulevards, I'm following an eerie homing signal toward some kind of a spiritual center. *"Turn here." "Don't turn there."* The power seems to center around a specific group of buildings in Brookside.

Border Star Elementary School   *Brookside shops Kansas City*

Memories are triggered. A simple diamond design on the Bryant Grade School, conjures a most familiar association. For some reason when I think of sweaters, or an Ivy League College, I always think of the Bryant School.

"When I see a prism of light through a window, I think of the reflective porch doors from a former home on Huntington."

"When I see Brookside Boulevard, I see Germany and a spirit that filled a Nazi experience."

Streetcars always close, somehow connected to the Temple, and a quest for Zionism. A most prevailing *"us-versus-them mentality,"* describing those who surround our neighborhood.

I realized that these recollections are *"their thoughts,"* not mine. That's what's so strange.., I am feeling thoughts of those who have lived before me! I am only here to absorb the aura.

Somehow, I have climbed inside their heads. Not of one individual, but a whole group bound together by me. All Independent from my own thoughts, yet still very much alive!

My only course has been to reflect against what has been presented to me. Always uniquely my own thoughts, yet, somehow bouncing against a historical backdrop that has shaped my very existence. *"It was all planned for me."*

For me personally, I know that I am more than the sum of my current awareness. I have innate instinctual reactions to things that were never introduced but could often feel.

I recognize that certain stimuli such as buildings, language, sounds, smells, and emotions, are from a vantage that often transcends my current experience.

I suppose that's why human beings in general, take such fulfillment in the "arts" and *"subconscious awakening!"*

My instincts tell me that Brookside was a type of vortex for me. It dragged a spirit even *"after"* the origin of my birth. It seems to attach many elements from a history I never knew, but could often feel.

A deeper interpretation is that, I once spoke German, and *"may"* have been part of a German Nazi experience.

I recognize great anxiety and yet excitement over similarities of German culture. Surprisingly, I have a kind of fond memory-type-of-experience from such stimuli. What should be sad and horrific, seems to take on a pleasant and comforting memory quality.

The recollections are not specific but rather emotional in nature. It's experienced in feelings of emotional perceptions like happiness, warmth, contentment, love, and struggle. All these elements have influenced my character.

"I am the product of culture that has genetically and spiritually bound me together through the evolution of time." Perhaps my spiritual flow leaped a few decades to an experience I know today. Without hesitation, speculation, or science, there are just some things you *"simply know!"*

It is those very emotions that have shaped the essence of my being. *"My attitude and inspiration!"* I believe personalities and motivations are derived from such ancient stimuli.

Interestingly enough, observations can also be made of other companion souls as they navigate through their journeys. Like a mirror or an aura, those tuned-in can pick up outside energy, and make incredibly accurate assessments of other people, their travels, and motives.

It appears that people radiate energy, and we have learned to detect such energy as a mechanism for survival. For whatever reason, it seems clear that some people have a stronger aura than others. *"I don't know why!" Perhaps it's a consequence of practice.*

In one example are three brothers.

One is trying to find his soul, one has lost his soul, and one is guided by his soul. Those who know them can attach who is who.

This makes no judgment of personality or value, but just an observation at another level. I certainly cannot explain such disparity from the same gene pool, but to only say, it appears to be true!

It is also observed that certain people can dampen energy off another and can suppress natural flow. It seems true that certain endeavors can enhance this connection and help tap raw talents passed from inner awareness.

Mind over matter seems to be relevant and a strong variable in the human condition. Under incredible stress, one can achieve uncommon feats.

Energy is contagious like yawning or a smile. The chemical balances of the psyche can randomly shift based off energy from another. Whole societies can shift based on energy of only a few. There is some kind of magnetic pull from individual to individual.

Emotions are waves

All emotions are waves that can be seen in brain activity recorded on an EEG. We receive millions of impressions daily and often in lieu of language. While we can't know its origin, we know these feelings exist in the background like a sixth sense.

Indistinguishable feelings regularly permeate our psyche. Buildings, places, and landscapes, often trigger these feelings. Negative experiences like combat-stress disorder, or a life-time of abuse, can also deeply affect our mindset.

We have been discussing the possibility, that emotions can be transmitted through our DNA. We should also consider that emotions could travel inside and outside the body. Perhaps, what we experience are simply echoes from elsewhere.

Our rearing and history shape our attitudes, but we also gain insight from unexplained sources. Thoughts and feelings are contagious, and are often propagate between individuals. Love is real. Perhaps there is something more going on here.

Strong experiences, such as persecution, can permeate our awareness, and perhaps be recalled from history. Does this mean we have experienced before? How is that possible?

Waves of any kind are projectable forever until it meets counter resistance. Such resistance is the result of competing waves, and then, only defined by observation. All waves are simply intervals in time.

If emotions can travel outside our biology, perhaps we regularly navigate through the dimension of time, only to be received and resurfaced again. Strong emotions reinforce pattern instincts and create a pervasive mindset. Something as horrific as a holocaust may never die. It may only re-materialize in biology at a later time.

We know hate can travel and spread, and so do our fears and ambitions. We create an environment of energy, and it affects the climate of everything within our grasp.

On the most micro-level, electrically charged waves affect the fabric of space-time. Those entrenched valleys can create channels of electrical charges that can carry our thoughts and fears. Such thought patterns are etched into the fabric of the cosmos perhaps forever.

Additionally, we know from the study of neuron networks, that repetitive or impactful experiences will enforce recall within the brain. It appears the brain carves instant recall channels as demonstrated through repetitive actions.

If the brain is physically changed by the experience, then perhaps it also is encoded in the DNA. This is another evolutionary function that might explain the passing of personality traits, fears, and tendencies through our future offspring. In essence, we have lived before.

Tracking the Journey

There are many observations about life that you know to be true, although it makes little logical sense...

An earlier statement that "Brookside was a kind of vortex for me" appears strange, because I was not born there. I was only nurtured there! My soul or "being" seems to be following me. My spiritual center drug my former essence, to this current place and experience I know today.

It appears these energy attachments, followed my path, and established my connection. I may have even chosen my exact partnering souls to experience life with.

Furthermore.., there is also the distinct possibility that I may have created those partnering souls as well.

I have identified (3) three very important and distinctive revelations. *One of the following may be true.*

> A. *I dragged my soul to this point in space/time, creating the person I know today.*
>
> B. *I somehow managed the partnering of my companion souls that are also very real and evolving through the cosmos with me, or.....*
>
> C. *I created my own relationships and partnering souls to suit my own motivations. (I created my own Universe!)*

In all three cases, I believe that the soul is directing the journey, and not necessarily the external force of a supreme being. A supreme being may be nurturing the flow, but that is also me *"a piece of the multiplex."* I have a definite hand in this direction.

As described in a recent book *"Seat of the Soul,"* read long after identification of such issues, it describes an *"ocean of universal energy."* Our souls are like a *"droplet out of the ocean"* containing all the properties of the entire entity. It sacrifices itself in the form of droplets of conscious energy that adapts to this experience. It maintains all the essence of the whole, as it recast itself into new *"assorted dramas."*

The purpose appears to be the resolution of unresolved issues that play out through an entire lifetime. It appears there are central themes that re-circulate over and over again, as the driving essence of the individual.

Through *psychoanalysis,* the essence of each person's life can be broken down into obvious themes. Those themes dictate the actions of a *"life-*

time school." Who to marry? What sexual motivation spins your sociality, friends, and workplace? What kind of work and play activities are in concert with your soul, and move you toward resolution of your re-defined essence.

I have recently discovered many of my own underling themes. Throughout my life, I have played out familiar and personal issues. Some too personal to express on the page, yet has shaped my ever-waking thought and identity. It influences my motivations and character. In reflection, I now understand that all my living experiences are pushed by a quest to resolve key central issues.

Anyone can identify his or her themes. It is present in such things as basic sexuality, your desires, and ongoing relationships. How some people make you feel, and how you position yourself throughout your life. *"What are your common themes?"*

A pattern begins to develop on how your life has been shaped by previous soulful encounters. Was I a prisoner? Did I die a horrific or unresolved death? Was I cast into an identity that follows my personality today?

Why do you suppose that people are fixed on specific forms of work, pleasure, and abuse?

The *"Seat of Soul"* written by *Gary Zukav,* also describes many of these same concepts and experiences. *(I must not be alone in this thinking).* In a most artful description of the power of self, he reveals these very enlightening truisms.

"That we are directed by a central spirit that transcends time and space as we know it."

"It has been and always will be the guiding force through our evolutionary process from awareness to awareness."

"That the sole has several unresolved issues that we seek to balance through the experiences of a lifetime."

"Those unresolved issues are the reason and core of why we live, how we react, and how we shape our existence."

"Those central themes tap our emotional responses and seek restitution."

"Actions that support our energy flow, create harmony and oneness of purpose."

"Actions that sever the natural flow is like a poison separating our personality from the direction of our soul."

I recognize that deep inside the soul is a much larger complex of conscious energy. This energy is tapped into the vastness of the Universe, yet is also specific to the individual.

My own experience seems to revolve around struggles, imprisonment, and a thirst for what is beyond the curtain.

This supports a type of mentality that manifests itself, over and over, through curiosity, imagination, and invention. Today, I seem to be in a type of holding pattern to better reflect and evaluate those underlying issues.

What kind of physical reality do I find myself in? This place and environment, dictates a type of pre-design presence before my time. Yet, I also realize that I am in control of this energy flow.

"It was I.... that established this order of which I am now to experience."

Dimensional Dynamics

Dimensional dynamics define our Universe. The Universe is both fluid and all encompassing … yet bonds itself through a variety of interdependent connections.

Travel through the cosmos is more likely an occurrence of dimensional elasticity, rather than our narrow three or four dimensional comprehension.

"We are stick figures on a two-dimensional page of paper, with no appreciation for the sky above or the desk below. From our limited vantage, we are babes in the woods, crying for a genesis to connect our souls."

As we develop new technologies and greater appreciation for the world within our dimension, we continue to sense the reality of planes just beyond our grasp.

Our dreams become volatile time capsules. Our memories are fluid adventure of lifetimes, moments, and perceptions, while we as humans, have difficulty separating the intervals of our own reality...........

— M Z

REINCARNATION

I have lived before...

Describing the concept of life and death is very complicated. *"Reincarnation"* holds many different interpretations as well. The statement that I have lived before is true, however not necessarily in a traditional sense.

It is not that I have lived before in this *"particular world,"* or even that I could find my former self in a past life. But rather,

I can live many dreams, and experience many lives, as I venture into varied experiences irrelevant to this timeline. That's kind of what we do when we dream…

There is no such thing as linear time, because time is an illusion. And if time is an illusion, then life may be an illusion as well.

My space and time are not your space and time. One's lifetime may not connect to another, or combine with another in the same living experience.

Instead, we move through other awareness via alternative dimensionality. Each experience is a new path of alternative reality, absorbed and focused by your personal soul. A lifetime of experiences is shaped by soulful drift. And that drift lives on indefinitely to take on new forms and creations. This describes a type of multi-verse.

By a quantum approach to consciousness, when we leave this world, we spread our knowledge to the rest of the Universe to be reabsorbed. Yet, a pattern maintains itself in the form of a conscious network. So, consciousness may be nothing more than a quantum relationship of correlated energy.

That network might be derived from a central spine. And that spine branches out from some kind of central authority. That authority is likely directed by your master will. And that *"will,"* is morphed and diluted as it experiences each branch of awareness.

So, once again, we come back to the central argument of a universal spirit. *"This might be the best explanation that the lord is one, but I'm not sure that's what theologians had in mind!"*

In this concept, there is a Universal spirit of many branches. Those branches live out multiple versions of reality. The central question is, are we talking about a collective soul with many spokes.., or are we talking about one central voice guided by an individual spirit that is *"self"* identified, and self- created.

Are other people's awareness as relevant as yours? Do they live in awareness apart from yours? Or, does my voice speak for all that's in my Universe? All strong questions......

It is possible to live many lifetimes from an isolated perch, distinct and separate from all other timelines. There may not be past or present, but instead life is experienced in a unique and volatile realm of existence.

"Quantum physics tells us that nothing that is observed, is unaffected by the observer. That statement from science holds an enormous and powerful insight. It means that everyone sees a different truth, because everyone is creating what they see."

—NEALE DONALD WALSCH

Who invented Who?

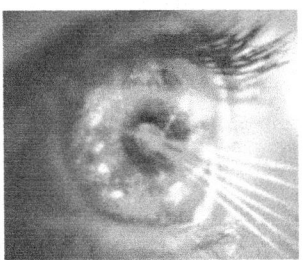

We have been talking about the possibility that I invented my own Universe. And if that is so, then I must have invented my father and my entire lineage as well.

We have discussed how the DNA genome evolves and adapts from not only the environment, but from our *"cultural environment"* as well. Certain repetitions, sayings, echoed fears and ambitions, all contribute to evolving our minds in a specific and dynamic way.

We are reared with a specific philosophy and mindset. That's why our social biases remain so strong. We inherit physical capabilities and mannerisms that seem to flow from offspring to offspring. Our physical order and experiences, dictate our identity as well as our historic aura. And those influences build on our ongoing living awareness.

While there seems to be familiarity to relationships, it is unclear if they are self-created, or part of a line of spiritual adaptation through the eons. Am I a product of my lineage, or is my lineage the product of my own creation?

Perhaps that *"familiar quality"* is simply the result of my own fabrication. My parents are perhaps only components of my own spirit. And, if that lineage is only fabrication, then seeking lost love ones, is moot indeed. On the other hand, if I am the product of ancestral extension, then their essence continues to live on inside me.

When I started writing this book, I favored a more traditional theory, where competing spirits meet, and converge in a kind of spirit world. The concept of *haunted houses* or *ghostly encounters,* describes a place where spooks live and survive, in a kind of outside spirit Universe.

As I have progressed in my analysis, I have moved to the conclusion that there are not necessarily independent and multiple entities in the Universe, but rather a singularity of flow.

There is either one central authority with many forks and branches that intertwine, **or** just one central authority that casts all relationships. Everything is directed from the same source.

So, in answering the question, **"Where are the dead now?"**

They are *"inside of us,"* not *"out there,"* and intertwined within a combined awareness.

The concept of oneness with the past, calls into question the concept of linear time and physical locality. As science is now discovering, location is never certain, and the essence of our material world is totally elusive. When we think, we process all aspects of our conversation. And when we dream at night, we invent the players and the drama that is yet to unfold. A super intelligence seems to be directing our actions, and that entity continues to be explored.

TANGENT REALITY

"We never experience anything other than the inside of our own consciousness."

—RUBERT SPIRA

"I regard consciousness as fundamental. I regard matter as derivative from consciousness. Everything that we talk about, everything that we regard as existing, postulates consciousness."

—MAX PLANCK

"The observer creates the reality."

—R.C. HENRY

Traditional reincarnation theory describes where one life passes on to another, and the soul takes another form on earth. One is reborn into a new identity, as the soul continues through our familiar arrow of time. This supports the electrical wave concept, as described on page 177, where electro-magnetism affects the flow of soulful energy. Matter and energy flow together, and regularly pass through bubbles and distortions throughout the Universe. This theory explains how the soul might migrate through various identities and time frames.

A variation of traditional reincarnation theory is what I call "Individualized Tangent Reality." The soul is reinvented in a fresh multi-dimensional Universe. The soul splinters into parallel or alternate realities. Awareness is the catalyst of its own construct. We build alternative timelines.

We live in separate and independent worlds from each other. Souls might touch in time and space, but we are all on very separate journeys. It's possible that we interact with ongoing soulful partners throughout our experience, however each journey is very much on its own. This could explain familiarity of relationships.

There is also a strong case to be made that there is just one central soul that derives all of consciousness. This has been described as Solipsism. Solipsism is the concept of being alone in the Universe, where one soul drives all of matter and reality. All of reality exists within one's mind. It is the observer that constructs time and the material world.

Another concept is known as Biocentrism, where there is consciousness as a result of biological uniqueness. Each living entity creates its own unique awareness. In a way, this describes Solipsism, but is created by each independent entity. Every living plant, thing, and creation, has its own special consciousness.

Experimental Evidence

Today's science is providing evidence, that consciousness is "not" derived from the material brain as once believed. The brain is not the incubator of awareness, but instead acts as a conductor of outside conscious energy. All material form may derive consciousness, from outside of our physical realm.

Great insight has been gained from near death experiences, where consciousness has been demonstrated after brain death. Audible experiments, along with signage hidden from patients, have revealed remarkable recollection. This could only be achieved by outside body experience. Awareness appears to be individualized, and is some kind of projection outside our biological form.

Quantum mechanics has demonstrated in the laboratory, that the material world is a function of *"probability" and not a stable reality.* Our observation triggers a materialistic construct that defines our awareness. It is consciousness that awakens all definition of matter.

Quantum mechanics reveals, that atomic particles only exist as waves of potential. When we make an observation, we define locality and assign definition to matter. This evidence is routinely confirmed in science, and is further described in the following examples:

1. The Double Slit Experiment has demonstrated that observation can affect the behavior of photons. Matter is not real until it is observed. The natural state of the Universe is only a range of "probabilities." The act of observing makes reality choose a conclusion. Scientists describe this as the *"Collapse Wave Theory."* It also appears that particles can move back and forth in time and recreate its own conclusion. The *Double Slit Experiment is further described on page 85.*

Scientists have centered around (4) key explanations for these strange results. All leading theories however, suggest mystical and strange conclusions that have shaken our fundamental understanding of reality to its core.

1a. The "**Copenhagen interpretation**," supports that all things are a result of a probability wave. Location and position of matter can never be defined or directly observed as noted by the "uncertainty principle."

This concept supports the idea of a "wave-particle duality," and that the wave function collapses, as a result of making a measurement. Observation defines its outcome. Particles can be in two states at once. This poses many ramifications for reality, and is the leading explanation in science today.

Schrodinger's Cat is both dead and alive!

1b. "Many Worlds Theory," differs in that it does not force the collapse of the wave function as result of observation. Instead, an object does all possible outcomes and creates actual splits in the Universe. Each new outcome creates its own special dimensional reality. Each action fans into all possible realities.

1c. "Many Interacting Worlds Theory," is an offshoot of the "Many Worlds Theory." It suggests that instead of multiple and separate worlds, they overlap and occupy the same time and space simultaneously. These parallel Universes interact with each other and create a multi-verse.

A "Cold Spot" discovered and analyzed by Durham University in 2015, supports this theory. Astrophysicists have discovered a strange barren area in the Universe that is much colder than the rest of space. It seems to be missing about 10,000 stars.

This cold spot, 2 billion light-years across, is a huge region that contains 20 percent less matter than it should. This has baffled scientists since its discovery. This suggests we may have adjacent or overlapping Universes, where gravity and its influence regularly exchange. Thus, dimensions may affect each other.

1d. "Pilot Wave Theory," says that objects radiate a "wave field," and are attracted to regions pre-determined by direction of particles and energy. We simply can't know all the hidden variables that affect its locality. Each particle follows its own deterministic trajectory, guided by a wave of unknown origin. Perhaps the newly discovered "Higgs Field" will help give better answers to this mysterious unknown wave.

Energy carves a predetermined path, likely forced by gravity on the fabric of space itself. The problem is, this theory does not describe the interchangeability of results. This was originally the leading theory, however, recent experiments have largely dispelled this conclusion. "Pilot Wave" theorists, continue to search for unknown variables that would explain the quantum's unpredictable behavior.

Other clues from "Quantum Mechanics," demonstrate other strange and variable qualities in measuring our reality.

2. Quantum Entanglement demonstrates a correlation between particles that can be light years apart. This would suggest that the fabric of time and space is interconnected through dimensional shortcuts. Space and distance may only be an illusion, as we might be living in a two-dimensional realm, but only perceiving a three-dimensional world. This has been described as a "Holographic Universe." This theory gives rise to the thinking, that all we experience may actually be derived from consciousness, not matter.

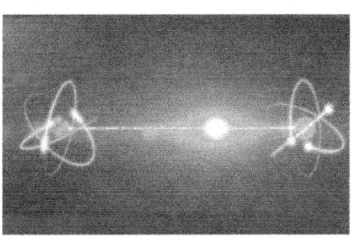

3. Quantum tunneling shows that particles move in and out of existence on a regular basis. Where do they go? It is believed that they share multiple dimensionalities, as does perhaps gravity. We live between dimensions and may also be connected through multiple time frames. This suggests our linear existence is not as it appears. Our consciousness may be fueling our awareness, and exceeds our understanding of time and space.

4. Evidence of Dark Matter & Dark Energy demonstrate that 95% of our physical Universe, is not interactive with us at all. We know "Dark Matter" exists, but this seems to be outside our normal physical Universe. It may affect the here and now through gravity, but has no direct impact on physical matter.

This shows more evidence that our three-dimensional world is only a small slice of our true physical reality.

5. "Superstring Theory," is currently the most popular concept of the Quantum world. Superstring suggests, we live in a nine-dimensional multi-verse, with extra dimensions curled up within ours. Nothing in our Universe is substance, but rather strings of energy that vibrate inter-dimensionally. Vibration is the incubator of all matter as we live among vibrating strings.

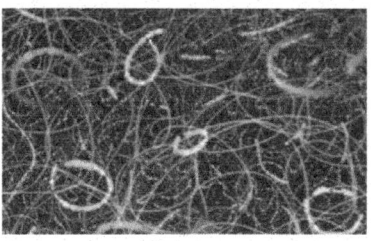

The math seems to support nine dimensions to account for the imbalance of gravity that we observe. It seems to solve the "Grand Theory of Everything," where the inconsistencies in "Quantum Mechanics" and "Relativity" are resolved.

6. "Simulation Hypothesis," considers the evidence of a computer-generated reality. More and more analogies seem to support what we observe in the Quantum world. The Quantum world behaves as if space and time is totally moot. All points are equal distance, and everything to its smallest scale is quantized. That would make sense if our Universe were more like a probability-based simulation, a computer, virtual reality, or a video game.

The Fibonacci code may have some relevance to what we see in nature. There appears to be hard programming in nature, and we all live within the restrictions of our programming.

7. The "Hadron Collider," at Cern Switzerland, is designed to accelerate particles at near the speed of light. Through observing its collisions, scientists have documented new and strange phenomena about the fabric of space. The recently discovered Higgs Boson lends credibility to the potential of a multi-verse. This accelerator has produced microscopic black holes, perhaps punching into alternative worlds.

8. Studies in dream research, past life experiences, and Parapsychology, have revealed new theories on the volatility of reality. Dr. Sam Parnia, New York State University, has conducted cutting-edge research comparing accounts of near-death experiences. There is remarkable consistency in patient accounts. Specific sounds during cardiac arrest, along with strategic images facing the ceiling, have demonstrated unusual recollection. Near death experiences, seem to follow a familiar pattern of light and consciousness, outside of the body.

Dr. Ian Stevenson, University of Virginia has researched dreams, reincarnation, and regression therapies. He has studied over 3,000 cases of children who recall having past life experiences. His team has presented evidence that such children have unusual abilities, illnesses, phobias, and obsessions, which could not be explained by environment or heredity alone. Parapsychology, is an established field of study at several universities around the world, focusing on improbable chance, and mind over matter experiments.

9. Intuition by religion. All known religions throughout history have wrestled with the concept of death and the afterlife. It appears to be ancient wisdom by intuition, that mankind has always gravitated to religious beliefs, and the eventuality of the soul. Just as we acknowledge intuition as a component of survival, we cannot overlook the propensity of humans, to infer life-after-death and the power from within. That consistency, throughout history, should merit serious recognition and consideration.

The above examples are evidence that our physical world is not as it appears. Observation and alternative dimensionality, affects matter pure and simple. Human beings are better defined by their consciousness, which channels energy through their perceived biological form.

Just as we have demonstrated how each person perceives a different interpretation of events, we also recognize each observation can be altered, bent, and interpreted differently. We can extrapolate that each person probably sees a very different world. We have our own unique dreams, and our own construct of how we perceive reality.

The other night, I observed my dog having an intense dream. Her leg continued to bang a nightstand for several minutes, as she appeared to be running or chasing something.

I could never begin to guess what her dreams might be about, but to say that it is clear that animals do dream. They paint their own alternative realities, and I'm sure that each animal paints its own individual construct.

So, if animals dream, do you suppose that insects also dream? Perhaps plants? Perhaps, even inanimate objects may have memory, and experience their own altered state.

I am sure their time references would be quite different from ours.

In the "Tangent Reality Concept," consciousness is forever ongoing. Our living experiences, shape our reality in a maze of wave potential and alternative timelines. Thus, when we describe reincarnation, we likely are fabricating awareness from a wide range of personal assorted dramas.

Another factor in our dramas, is that time appears to be flexible and dynamic. We know that our senses interpret "now" at very different times. Our brain always has delays in decoding sensory impressions being perceived. Thus, we are always experiencing the past, and stitching together a new concept of what we call "now."

The fact that "time" may be an illusion, means that we may be experiencing simultaneous experiences, and in a variety of order. If I lived the Nazi German experience, it might be nothing more than a manifestation of a unique timeline, experienced by my own subconscious.

Life dramas, such as the one I'm living now, may simply be a tangent reality. My father, or someone who was living in that same period might experience a completely different universe. Today I joke that the election of Donald Trump is nothing more than an alternative reality that we fell into. Perhaps at some point, we will rejoin the former timeline, and correct the course of the Universe.

Another Dream, Another Horizon

While the "Many Worlds Interpretation" is a leading theory that describes the splintering of reality, I further suggest, that instead, we might actually be living in the "Many Interacting Worlds" Interpretation. The mind is an inventive and dynamic interpreter of reality. We experience personalized shifts in consciousness, perhaps inspired by overlapping dimensions.

As described earlier, nothing is more revealing than our own dreamscape. We construct full episodes of awareness from a multitude of familiar and unfamiliar settings. In a sense, we are truly the rulers of our own Universe.

I will describe yet another dream, demonstrating how intense detail makes an unmistakable impression. Our minds have tremendous capability to invent specific and structured reality. Described below, is my "Night at the Furniture Store."

Night at the Furniture Store

"Recently I found myself in a line at a theater. The theater was actually owned by a relative of mine, but he was not there. The carpet is red, and the walls were baby blue. The room smelled of popcorn.

There is a small crowd, just 7 people. One man was white, about age 40, by himself, and the others came together and were of Indian descent. I believe there were four men and two women. All appeared to be in their mid 20s and ready to party, as if they had come from some kind of a celebration.

For some reason, we all loaded into a green van on Valentine Boulevard in Kansas City, and then later boarded an older entertainment boat for a tour. As we sat on the upper deck, we watched as the boat arrived at the dock with a large parking lot behind it. We then boarded that same van again, where I had left a newspaper on the back-left seat of gray leather upholstery. The seatbelt was frayed. I felt the cold metal buckle holding it in my hand, as the edge seemed to scratch my index finger.

Our driver was of middle eastern descent, and drove only a short drive across the parking lot, where we were in route to a large furniture store. As we parked, I noticed a corner appliance store where my father had worked. I yelled from the parking lot, "Hey your doors are still locked." His part-ner Jerry, now deceased, opened the door, turned on the storefront sign, and waved thanks.

We continued to the mega Furniture Store on foot through the broken parking lot, and got in line under a large yel-low sign.

I couldn't make out the letters, but it had blue trim and was at least four stories high. Inside, we saw bowling alleys and a wide range of entertainment options. I was asked to play, but

I declined one of my co-passengers.

As I sat firmly on the western-styled horned-chair with cow-hide seats, I talked with an older woman named Charlotte. She had just arrived from Omaha, and held a large black shopping bag with gold stars. She discussed her niece, but I really wasn't listening. As she got up to leave, she greeted a middle age man named George. I assumed he was her son.

As I sat in the chair, I gazed at the massive chandeliers and the wooden structure of the ceiling. The office to my left had long white counters, and was messed up with considerable papers. The backdrop of the office looked to be a light oak.

I was then asked by an employee, "how long I planned to be there." Then I woke.

This is only one example of multiple dramas I experience on a nightly basis. There actually was much more detail that I had forgotten. I don't know why we usually forget our dreams, but certain elements do seem to leak through. It is obvious we seem to touch, taste, feel, and smell the experiences we are creating. For in this environment, the reality is as real as the one we are currently experiencing.

We constantly scan our awareness during waking hours as well. We have multiple interpretations of daily encounters, but seem to hold a consistency of construction during those waking hours. One thought leads to another, and seem to spring from previous encounters.

In viewing the "Many Worlds Concept" of a splintered Universe with all possible consequences, I find it more likely that we aren't splintering these choices. But instead, we are choosing a construct from our own thoughts. This describes a type of "Holographic Universe" where our thoughts project the environment. Matter as we know it is simply a mental construct.

This describes a type of "Tangent Reality." One of the most interesting questions posed is; "can we re-create our tangent reality?" Are we able to reconstruct the past, or relive a relationship with a deceased loved one?

The unfortunate answer is no. The memories that we launch from our past, is simply a former fabricated construct. We can't relive the past, because it was no more real than the current construct we are currently inventing. We can reinvent and morph a new relationship with the past, but we can never retrace the same construct that was manufactured in the first place.

Did someone actually ever live?

It's a good question. All former reality ceases to currently exist. Our physical Universe has changed. Our construct has been renewed. We are regularly reinventing our Universe.

THE NEVER ENDING DREAM

The Never Ending Dream Theory or NED, describes heaven and the afterlife as a series of ongoing dreams, where time has no meaning, and one lives in a realm of unlimited consciousness.

This theory calls into question assumptions of a traditional Universe or a biblical afterlife. Instead, perpetual dreaming may well be our natural state.

In a recent book titled *"Proof of Heaven,"* by Dr. Eben Alexander, he describes his own near-death experience. "Within dreams my mind can almost instantaneously paint beautiful landscapes, design and decorate rooms, create new faces, and compose dialogues worthy of a movie script."

"A static heaven of timeless wonder, love, and adventure may be the best and most plausible explanation, that a merciful God can give his creatures."

Jacobs ladder describes a bridge to heaven through his dreams. Perhaps that may be the authentic gateway to our own heaven.

"There is amazing capability of the mind, to create intricate dreams."

As we drill deeper into the concept of a never-ending dream, we continue ask ourselves, who is directing the drama. Is the dream a product of our own creation, or is it the product of external forces? Those forces can be either partnering souls in a stream of awareness, or just one central supreme force.

If we conclude that it is a fixed central source that guides our activities, then we must ask the question, "are we controlled by an ultimate creator, or by higher beings?" Perhaps, it is our future selves in a kind of computer simulation.

The *"Holographic Universe"* describes a Universe where all information, *"everything"*, is captured on a two-dimensional surface. We are simply experiencing a three-dimensional world as part of a grand illusion. Such a concept further suggests that information is moved in a kind of computer- generated program. Consciousness rules all of humanity.

The ramifications of such a program would imply limited free-will, as directed by an unknowable grander source. Perhaps that grander source is what we mistake for God.

Instead, I rather trust that our heaven offers the ultimate free-will. We as our own entity can only create that perfect world.

"The Universe is in our hands."

While I would like to believe it is "we" directing the journey, there are so many unknowns, that it doesn't seem quite plausible. We just happened to arrive on the scene, and are driving the bus, but we have no idea who we are, or where we are going.

Perhaps we do experience a kind of biological blindness, as we navigate through our human existence. The NED theory suggests, that we are born again, and will be released from our conventional bodies.

But released to do what? Do we shackle ourselves in a kind of spiritual workout? *"More weights please, or with most of our knowledge tied behind our backs!"*

There seems to be a direction, and it would seem we also take part in this process *thankfully*. Perhaps something is pushing the boat, but the illusion is that we hold some kind of control of the rudder.

All good questions as we crystallize ideas that are passed through the generations. We establish *"hard truths"* that balance the questions of humanity, until our children stretch their own ideas of the cosmos.

In my version of reality, I have chosen to believe in my own free-will. I make the decisions, and provide all the answers.

And that may well be the most ultimate illusion of all.

Synchronicity vs Elastic Universe

There are two schools of thought on the operations of our Universe. You could describe these positions as **"will,"** or **"free will."**

1. Those who see a world ruled by **synchronicity** tend to follow a *"Newtonian point of view."* The concept of **"will"** is the natural coarse of our Universe. Most religions conceptualize a grand "watchmaker" who sets the world in motion, and has a definitive hand in cause and effect.

Personality types who fall in this camp generally prefer "order," and find it painful to live in a world of variables and uncertainty.

2. Those who gravitate to an **Elastic Universe** concept, see a dynamic and flexible world as described in "Quantum physics" and "relativity." Everything is variable, and cause and effect have limited meaning. The human soul has maximum **"free will"** to create and shape its own destiny.

Those who fall in the "Elastic Universe" camp may find the dogma of order and restrictions, most confining and imprisoning.

There is a natural propensity to fall into one of these two groups. These two divisions highlight fundamental differences in theology and our conception of the world.

Generally speaking, right brained individuals *(Those dominated by their creative side,)* tend to fall into an elastic Universe philosophy. Left brained individuals, *(described as linear thinkers, engineers, etc,)* would have a natural tendency to find comfort in more order.

This doesn't mean personality traits won't cross over. They do. But generally speaking, crossover is usually due to environmental influences in rearing. From the Myer Briggs personality profile, an **"ENFP"** would fall nicely into the Elastic Universe Camp, while an **"ISTJ"** would find comfort in Synchronicity.

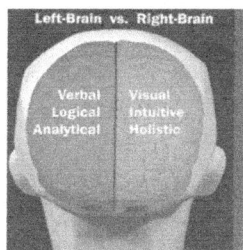

"We are what we think!"

"It has been shown that people of higher IQ, are easier to hypnotize and mind control than more creative individuals. People with lower IQs, are less likely to be mesmerized than formally educated persons with advanced degrees."

—*THOMAS SHERIDAN*

Religious Understanding

"What to tell the Children"

After discussion of various belief systems covering religion and reality, the question remains what to tell our children.

Religion serves many functions. It bonds a community and provides a sense of belonging and engagement. One purpose is to provide structure and *"easy communicable"* answers in a world entangled with possibilities and dynamic reality. Here are some basics that should be assigned to our fundamental beliefs.

- **Every person has a right and duty to get to heaven.**

  What ever your definition of heaven, each person must carve out their own map and create their own ideal. Mankind is free to dream and imagine their own Universe, and that freedom, is the ultimate key given by the creator. Like the laws of nature, survival depends on a quest for understanding, and the obtainment of knowledge. A broken spirit wont survive, but an expanded one will. The promised land is in front of us, and this journey defines us all.

- **One can find heaven through deeds and enrichment, not necessarily in acceptance.**

Of many vehicles chosen, many worship a traditional concept of deity and oneness of God. Such basic structures have been enhanced for a variety of reasons. This is not always religiously inspired. The church has acquired a central place in the lives of many followers. While some flourish in acceptance, many others are desensitized and led astray on their natural journey to heaven.

- **Jesus is a methodology to get to heaven.**

Just one of many vehicles. Much like our economic system, powerful lobbies and influences have monopolized their brand of religion. What should have thousands of natural gateways, has morphed into a handful of world dominated religions and hierarchies. It appears tradition holds a valuable status in society, and thus may blind us from obvious choices in logic. We are repetitive creatures and find comfort in familiarity and uniformity. I have known people truly inspired by a consistent word, and that vision delivers its own reality of heaven.

- **There can be heaven without hell.**

One, should be disillusioned by a punishing God. This violates a positive concept in nature and a supreme being. Not only should God rise above punishment and pettiness, but should be powerful enough to overcome forces of darkness. The contrast between heaven and hell is far too simplified based on the evidence of complexity in our Universe.

If Heaven is best described as *"enlightenment,"* then one can view life as a journey rather than condemnation.

- **We are not born sinners.**

Children are born in the grace of God. We were willed into existence either by a supreme force, or our own spiritual identity. In either case, we must share confidence that our process is one of purpose and enlightenment. We have been programmed to grow and flourish. To ask for forgiveness for being human, has little rationality. There is no sin in being born human. There is only purpose and agenda of which we explore our entire life.

After all is said, It is important to expose children to religious concepts and stimulate thinking. One should engage historical perspective of humanities, and develop moral ethics that best serve survival.

"It is important not to twist figurative translations into literal dogma. Nurturing should never be led through guilt!"

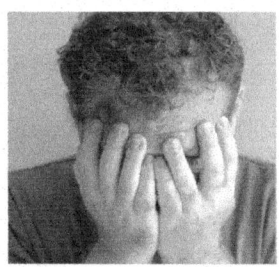

What does Heaven look like?

- Do you see your parents there?

- Will you have all the answers to the Universe?

- What will you do with your time? Will you play games?

- Will you re-live living experiences?

- Are you still responsible for decisions, choices of right and wrong?

- Are you sin free in heaven?

- Will you continue to be judged?

- If mental stimulation and challenges keep you entertained, will you have the chance to exercise this experience?

- What would paradise be like without challenges?

- Can paradise actually be achieved?

WHAT IS OUR TRUTH?

We seem to live in a matrix of overlapping Universes, as we rely on the human body to limit our focus from a vast echo.

Because our being can live in any time we choose, we never actually die, but rather progress through an assortment of chosen dramas. Our soul is at the heart of our journey as we meander through a range of cosmic existences.

One factor in our evidence is that matter around us weaves in and out of existence all the time. We further recognize that time and space is completely relative, and as such, we must also acknowledge the flexibility and dynamics of our human entity. We secure clues that we live in a maze of dimensional overlays, and those overlays separate our experience from awareness to awareness.

When we dream we live through a thousand lifetimes. Each dream not necessarily related to the next. But there seems to always be a common thread. *"It is always you."* And it usually has some kind of *"common hook"* into your other realities.

In the dream state, time has never been more elastic. Its often difficult to separate a memory from what is about to happen next. And that *"idea incubator,"* seems to run through a central personal resource described as your subconscious.

> *"The dream is a small hidden door to the deepest and most intimate sanctum of the soul."*
>
> —CARL JUNG

"Truth in Science," and *"Truth in Nature,"* is skewed from the perspective of the participant. That participation follows its own coarse of individual vantage in time and place.

As does the graviton and our smallest quantum particle, we too would be able to pass between a mesh of dimensional walls, if we only were small enough to do so. The stretch of time, places us in many places at once and in within many alterations of our existence.

So, as we continue our search for the heavens, we must recognize that the heavens already encompass us. Our journey is never a destination but rather an ongoing relation-ship with a multi-dimensional world.

And perhaps our mission is to narrow the ground clutter, and experience a world that perpetuates its own reality. Humans have a perspective vastly different from any other life form on earth, and vastly different from anything else of material existence around us. That uniqueness defines us as humans, as we *"construct"* a focused path of existence.

In our world, there is no up or down, here or there, past or present, or even a tangible physiology that we can hang on to. It just is, and we think because we are.

And the ultimate truth in our Universe is shaped by our own soul. And that seems to be the true window of our cosmos, and perhaps the only real voice of God.

MICHAEL ZEMBROWSKY
2020

VIBRATION OF THE UNIVERSE

Addendum

Vibration of the Universe

"Music as a distinct dimension of time."

In our physical world, some might conclude that the refraction of light is what constructs our physical reality. Much like quantum particles require a Higgs field to give it mass, every-thing in the Universe is relative, and dependent on what it's reflected against. Without reflection, nothing exists.

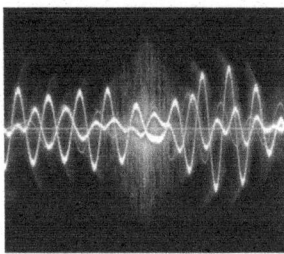

Sound acts as an independent conduit on its own separate plane. Without sound, auditory reality or its subsequent vibration has no meaning. All information relies on its own channel of delivery. Its through interpretation that we shape our awareness.

While sound waves require air to fulfill the definition of sound, all waves continue forever by a range of unique carriers. "We are all aware of the process of converting sound waves into *"electromechanical oscillators,"* (Radio Signals), that span on forever.

Vibrations fill the fabric of space/time, and generate unique signatures that stretch throughout the cosmos. Music is one of many delivery systems that shape our current reality. Each signature is affected by the medium conducting it, and the vantage of those receiving it.

"Music can be described as existing in many places at once, and having many different faces."

—ARETHA KLEINMAN

Vibrations rule the world of string theory as each oscillation carves its own definition in time and space. We are just now discovering how frequencies are the essence of all physical matter. Everything in the Universe is a result of waves, and emits its own unique pattern throughout the cosmos.

Music delivers emotions and ideas that form unique bridges of perception. Most enlightening is that it is *"personal"* for each one of us. People draw associations, and those feelings influence distinctive patterns in our cerebral cortex.

Music can influence appeasement, calming the wild, agitation, or aggression as demonstrated by war drums. Sound can generate physical adrenaline, aggressiveness, melancholy, or relax the subconscious while releasing endorphins and certain muscle groups in the body.

Craving a familiar sound niche, conjures perceptions of primal emotions. The essence of our survival often relies on *"fight or flight,"* and emotion brought out by audio stimulation.

Music delivers an essential defense mechanism that can intertwine history with current reality, and is essential for navigating choices into the future.

Music Therapy

Music therapy is the science of affecting mood and chemical balances in the brain. Addictive and stimulating sound can enhance mental wellness, and promote better alignment with nature. Sound promotes creativity, and allows a person to travel to both *"vast"* and *"familiar places."*

Just as human IQ is transmitted from one offspring to the other; established patterns in the brain are also imprinted and emulated in our evolutionary process.

Emotional temperament seems to be passed down as well. We further recognize that electrical charges in the brain are also affected by outside stimulus. Electrical patterns in the brain are transmittable, and produce their own carrier signals.

Of the billions of vibration received everyday, such signals are stretched and delivered through time. Waves continue forever, and that property alone impacts the volatility of our perception. *"Voices carry forever, and such voices often inspire creativity in the here and now."*

"How McCartney said that the entirety of the melody and chord progressions of "Yesterday" —one of the most covered songs of all-time —came to him upon waking from a dream."

"How Lennon said that songs would sometimes mysteriously appear to him at 3 a.m., and if he didn't get up and commit the idea to tape and/or paper, he simply would not be able to rest again."

We understand that time and space are intertwined in nature. Just as we seek security in shelter, comfort, and protection, we too seek waves of energy that renew and refresh our consciousness. Music influences ideas and imagination, while also connecting a kind of bridge through time.

Each person draws their own association. If we listened to Bach growing up, we associate the very sections of the music with associated reality. Music is personal and dynamic for each person. Patterns have mental associations that connect memories, concepts, and personal aspirations.

We have also learned, that music is incredibly segmented. Nothing is more accurate and distinctive of audiences, than its genre that defines multiple stereo-types and subgroups. That is why advertisers place such stock in targeting audiences by genre.

Music separates age, income, lifestyles, and personalities most successfully, yet also can individualize the taste of each listener. *"No two people hear the same thing!"*

Music is connection from the soul, and its rhythmic patterns shape vivid emotions that shape awareness. Many melodies are inspired from a range of unidentifiable sources. Each creation paints its own feeling, vision, and perception, in a timeless source of experiences.

I've always maintained that Music is *"divinely inspired."* The most prolific songwriters and poets derive energy from the abyss, and generate ideas that construct a world vision. One key vehicle in transmitting these visions is the art of music.

"When music becomes an emotion, the audience is truly captivated, for it be a reflection of its creator's soul."
—Kathryn Marie Ligon

As a description of soulful understanding, I have developed several musical compositions that express my own personal journey through music. I hope you appreciate my window called the "Star Sitter."

ORIGINAL MUSICAL COMPOSITIONS

Songs written by
Michael Zembrowsky

Star Sitter

Pulling thy small molten self from the lava of evil
Expelling it to the bright haven of the stars
Driving towards the evolution of the star sitter
and in his seat driving to the next constellation in the stars

And once on the point of truth
will you know what to do
all the visions here are all so very good
We lift up our cups to speak
and toast this new odyssey
the lessons here are all so very good ....

Driving thy small molten self to the next destination
Cracking a seam, into the fabric of the stars
Driving to the evolution of the star sitter
and in his seat, unto the next generation in the stars

Power Dream

And once on the point of truth
will you know what to do?
Our values, our purpose, we have our reasons
Power-flight into the dead of the night
Cold-shift to what ever seems right
Our logistics, our power we have our reasons

Like the sunshine on the western horizon
our position is gloomed, our reasons seem true
And were screaming, reaching, always believing.........

But only we can make wings
for only we can dream
a thousand lifetimes lost in the heavens
And as our twilight evaporates
new horizons will dominate
The star child brain is well on his way
to his brighter days.

Black Star

Once I rose to a point of no religion
Confounded by tradition, sweeping-energy apart
Piercing the darkened-veil of a cosmetary curtain
Sweeping in a narrow-path toward a solitary star

Trapping-deep within, the circles of a travel-cone
Meeting-deep within, the frequency of heart
Stealth-madness, rushing through an open-gate
From this vantage-place, we're hostages of fate

Once I rose way beyond the stars
Blocking my connection trying to learn just who we are
Placing thy blackened face upon the corner of a window
Peering through the moments of our sedimentary parts

From any set of points we are hostages of speed
We simply cannot leave where time won't allow us to be.
Trapped deep within the fray, towards the center of the plane
tumbling in a circle, ordered by our fate.............

Valley of Roses

Dead are the ones who dreamed for the fight for freedom
Gone are the ones who were lost in the plight
And though their bodies lay in the valley of eternity
their being, their blood prints, always follow me........

And where are they now, what did they think,
was it pro-creation, or echoed fragments of me?

And the Valley of Roses must live and die for me
building from a distant past, and mending together my peace.
From Suvalk to Brookside, the visions are within me
In and out of phase like shattered pieces of me.....

It owns me now, like wreckage from the deep
It marks me now, like memories on a string......
Owns me now, like shackles from beneath
It raises me now, broken spirit message release

Another Horizon

As the sun soaks-up another horizon
It guides my stars through the night
Like a whisper of madness across an ocean of vastness
chasing the dreams of my life.

Won't you believe what it's destined to be?
Waiting for the curtain to fall ....
In a motion of blindness through the otherwise silence,
reaching for the weight of the stars

History tells us of another day passage,
rolling through the volumes of thoughts
In an ancient day vision we've cast our submission
trapped beneath the future in the dark

Riding on the edge of tomorrow
seeding the hope of the soul
Waiting in the shadows of-the fold,
lighting a path from the cold.

Intervals of Perception

The central light of my life remains open
It's a painted workshop for my wandering soul.......
It's about the moments of emotion and focus
Reading from the leafs that blow through my road

Intervals of motion breaking the day
Time shattered moments casting their way
Crying for the spirits to connect the soul
A measure of position, perceptions, and goals.....

Time captures memories of adventures and dreams
Separating the visions of my post-reality
Flashing through the moments of timeless scenes
Captured in awareness of the probabilities

SYNOPSIS

"Our reality is most relative. We create our own interpretations and create our own Universe. We nurture our spirit through a host of personal relationships."

"Reality is a projection in time, as we maintain guidance from the essence of our soul."

"We affect our Universe, as our Universe affects us."

"We exist in the mind of God before, during, and after our earthly experience."

"The human soul is light in the darkness, as we play a central role in constructing our realities. We are one with the creator."

—MICHAEL ZEMBROWSKY

Summary

In Search of the Heavens

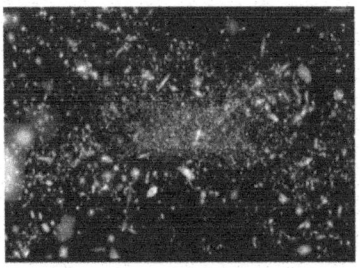

Preface

"*A look at intuition*"

There seems to be an ongoing presence throughout our Universe. It follows and shadows us throughout our life.

Preface 3

Part A

"*Religion and religious practices*"

We seek definition and meaning in a world confused by what we see. Some assume absolute knowledge from only a small vantage of truth. As we seek answers, we build a theology that accommodates our vision.

In Search of the Heavens 9

We seem to be traveling a great journey, and part of a much grander multiplex. *"Perhaps we are partners with the cosmos."* Or, *"perhaps we are simply the pawns of a supreme manipulator."*

OUR JOURNEY 12

"Evolution" appears to be our ordered process both spiritually and biologically. We are mandated to follow a natural order as we grow and develop as an entity. Our perspective is relative, but our natural instincts appear inherited. We also seem to gain insight from a time and place outside our Universe.

OUR JOURNEY 13

In the final scheme, there is probably no judgment at all, just a movement through a process. The trappings of tradition influence our religious practices, and may actually compromise spiritual growth. We follow a maze of ritual, often leading us nowhere.

"Perhaps heaven is best found through personal exploration, as opposed to contrived man-made methodologies."

FINAL JUDGMENT 22
TRAPPINGS OF TRADITION 23

From the minds of ancient Gods, we have experienced a rich history of myth and superstition. It influences our current ongoing theology.

Great philosophers have challenged the prevailing attitudes of their time, but have also incurred great persecution.

MINDS OF THE GODS 36—39

An overview of most religions demonstrates an obsession with judgment, and the eventuality of the soul. Definition of life and death holds many considerations, and is often manipulated by a host of man-made justifications.

CYCLE OF LIFE 41—44
TO LIVE OR DIE 45—47

Abraham, the father of three world religions, has led a trail to our modern monotheistic understanding. We have influenced genetic gene pools that have segregated into various cultures. The accounts in the Bible often raise more questions than it answers. Its credibility should logically be challenged!

ONE HUNDRED GENERATIONS 53—65

Part B

"Reality is Relative"

"Reality" takes on many perspectives, and is personal. Social influence finds its way into a common mindset, and forms its own brand of community awareness. Our physical world further skews our perceptions. We experience our earthly environment, within our own time frame, space, and existence.

REALITY IS RELATIVE 69—72

"A boy with a different angle can see anything he wants and project his illusions on to others. He forces us to question what we can actually count as our reality. Certainly not sight, sound, or touch."

WHAT ARE THE ANGLES 77-79

The quantum world sometimes confuses *"cause and effect,"* and *"dimensionality."* Time and locality are never certain. The Newtonian view of a synchronized world is challenged, as time and space prove most elastic. There are a vast range of potential outcomes for each and every event.

WHAT IS TOUCH 83—85

Only by our thoughts and awareness, do we ensure we are alive. The term alive has a multitude of meanings. Our true connection with the Universe may actually be *"thought,"* over *"substance."*

HOW WE KNOW WERE ALIVE 93—94

The **"Circle People,"** demonstrate how we might find ourselves in an altered state of reality, within a very different kind of Universe. We are evolving creatures both biologically, and within our own self-awareness. Our plugs to reality are often variable.

THE CIRCLE PEOPLE 97—100

We recognize how the current power structure has dominated our psyche and daily reality. Our mindset is often submission to prevailing wealth and power. We often slant our history, and define goodness as what best suits our motivations.

ILLUSION FOR CONTROL 107—109

Our physical environment skews our vantage of reality. We view the world in terms of up or down, past or present, and even living or dead. Through the cosmos, we discover that time and dimensionality, are ever expanding. With each new insight, we discover more and more mysteries…

VASTNESS OF LANDSCAPE 113—114
IN ALL THE COSMOS 121

In contemplating alien life, we estimate very little in common with our earthly existence. Our human biology seems to emulate that of a hard- wired computer, and evolution is more like a pre-designed script. *"Are we pawns of eternity, or active players in our own creative process."*

TOUCHING ALIEN WORLDS 124—127
OUR HUMAN MACHINE 129—133

When we dream, we invent our own Universe, and invent both sides of the dialogue. We live within an ongoing and flexible drama.

THE DREAMSCAPE 153

Our lineage also follows a migrating sense of reality. We are absorbed into a societal flow that moves and changes over time. Many aspects of our history fade into nothing more than ghostly images.

DRIFT OF SOCIETY 157—159

Part C

"Dynamics of the Soul"

"Time" is the great divider of our *version* of awareness. As demonstrated by variations of relativity, our perception of any event has its own skewed vantage.

Dynamics of the Soul 171—174

"Gravity" and elasticity of space will affect the passage of time, as molecules flow from one point to another. Such effects create time warps, bubbles, and distortions that influence the passage of history. *"As we meander through life, we experience a kind of interplay, chasing a dynamic soul."*

Time Transverses Awareness 175—176

A realization develops that we are more than the sum of our parts. We perceive ideas and instincts that have origins in our ancient past. Those origins shape our direction, and influence our hopes, dreams, and fears. *"Perhaps we have lived before."*

Time Transverses Awareness 177—179

We are part of a much larger complex of energy and influence. Multi-dimensionality truly defines our existence. We question who invented who, and *"if seeking the dead, is even relevant at all."*

Who invented Who 197—199

Tangent Reality describes a type of Reincarnation, where one lives many lives, as part of their own mental fabrication. The mind is flexible, and constructs the Universe. Science seems to imply this ultimate reality through quantum physics.

The Never-Ending Dream illustrates the potential of the mind, and its power in creating reality. Much like Jacob's ladder to heaven, our dreams may unlock the true volatility of our reality.

As we explore the value of religion, we question what heaven truly looks like. *We contemplate if paradise can actually be achieved.*

The Universe seems to have a vibration all its own. It conveys itself in many forms including the form of music. Music conveys emotion and often appears to be divinely inspired! Enclosed are examples of personal writings, through a window, I call the *"Star Sitter."*

In summary,

We challenge the nature of our truth. Truth in nature, and truth in science, is only relevant from the perspective of the participant. Our goal is to limit the ground clutter of human existence, and to find bridges that direct us along the journey. *"Those bridges should best lead us to our own version of heaven."*

WHAT IS OUR TRUTH 224—226